# Holy Shift!

## Driving Through Grief in a Vintage VW

**Michelle Le Brun**

Printed in the United States of America.



ISBN-13: 978-1-957651-27-9
Library of Congress Control Number: 2023900502

Designed by Rachel Valliere

INDIE BOOKS INTERNATIONAL®, INC.
2511 WOODLANDS WAY
OCEANSIDE, CA 92054

www.indiebooksintl.com

# Contents

*Third Gear:*

## Driver's Ed



*Fourth Gear:*

## The Road Map to Praying Mary Ellen's Rosary

# Dedication

To my divine road warriors: my sister Mary Ellen Le Brun, my uncle Fr. Frank Taney, and my dad Louis M. Le Brun, this book is your legacy. For the unexpected and untimely flat tires I experienced while envisioning and creating this book, I needed to look no further than the tools in my trunk. You three were my spiritual jack, the inflated spare tire, and the lug wrench; essential to getting back on the road. I am eternally grateful for the fix.

# Preface

*Go ahead and hop in.*

My car, that is. Take a ride with me as I share my family's story of being broken down, shifting through loss, and getting back on the road.

*Shift into first gear.*

I have found that experiencing loss is traumatic, enduring grief is lifelong, and writing about both is cathartically clumsy. I've been driving down this road for over fifty-three years. I would let you take the wheel, but it's a stick shift and difficult to navigate. There will be many starts, stops, and stalls. She's an antique, a classic, and holds great sentimental value with every mile. She has a history, the kind you never forget. Nor would you want to. I am the one registered and insured to drive this car. You, my friend, can ride shotgun.

*Shift into second gear.*

You can see everything I see through the windshield before you, but as the driver, my view is different. I am highly aware of everything in front of me and behind. I need to be alert, defensive, responsible, and prepared for anything that crosses my path. Expect unpredictable weather, unaware pedestrians, unforeseen roadblocks, an unassuming dog, or an uncertain driver. You never know what you will experience when you are driving through grief with your heart. We will cruise but have no control. You will be relaxed as the passenger and thanks for the company, by the way.

*Shift into third gear.*

I will be hyper-focused, and my periphery will be over-engaged as I anticipate imminent danger. Worry from loss can have me in overdrive sometimes. You may feel the effect of an unexpected speed bump but be relieved your muffler didn't suffer the consequences. By the way, we will not take the expressway. We will be driving down Route 1. The roads will be rough and the trip longer, but we will take it all in. The gas tank will sometimes be full, often on fumes, or empty altogether. Refueling is essential on this journey. We could break down in the middle of nowhere. Don't worry, a divine tow truck is always nearby. But you must summon it. We could get lost, and GPS is useless. Often the middle of nowhere has no Wi-Fi. We will waste energy with worry, but not for long. I have a road-tested and roadworthy navigational tool at my access 24/7; a spiritual compass that will point us in the right direction. True North waits for us in the distance. Keep driving.

*Shift into fourth gear.*

Be open to what comes. So much unexpectedness comes from unexpectedness. And although we don't drive the same car when we experience loss, you do, however, have to drive when it is your turn behind the wheel.

*So, take the keys.*

The loss is an agonizing moment. It's seen in the rearview mirror. The grief relentlessly comes at you in the windshield, like driving rain or a blinding snowstorm. Your wipers will help push the inclement weather away, and once again, your vision will be clear until the next storm hits. Your loss can be resembled in a moment or a marathon. What helped my family may help you. What you manifest in mindful prayer can be your road map to peace. The road is long, lonely, dark, and littered with distractions, until one day it's not, so much. Keep driving. *Keep shifting*. The one thing you can depend on during grief is that the sun always rises in the morning. Let it shine on your face. You deserve it after driving in the dark all night.

If life's circumstances have you off the grid and lost, there are many self-help books on grief written by educated therapists. I am not a trained professional. My training in loss and grief has been a lifelong personal research project that is difficult to footnote. I believe if you have something valuable to share with others along the bumpy road and the twists and turns of living with loss and grief, then I'm going to jump in the passenger seat with you and throw you the keys. Paying it forward is an essential human obligation.

*Buckle up.*

*And drive.*

*First Gear:*

# Broken Down

# 1 Test Drive Of Faith

The summer of '69 was driven with impossible possibility. There were test-drives of all kinds. In music, Woodstock rocked. In space, Neil Armstrong walked the moon. In war, Nixon began to bring our troops home from Vietnam. Life's highway was paved with hope. In July of that summer, my parents, Louis and Alice, took our family of six on a road trip of our lives. It was to be a cross-country vacation of a lifetime. Nothing could have prepared us for the unexpected detour we would soon face—the impossible possibility that would end in unimaginable tragedy. It would be a test drive of our faith and hope proving essential to our survival as a family.

When my parents told us their grand plan, my older sister, Mary Ellen, my two older brothers, Dave and Steve, and I were beyond excited. My dad was the most committed father, and we never took a back seat to his work. He was the owner of a fledgling automobile dealership. It would flourish in time, but in 1969, he was getting his bearings. So perhaps it was a little excessive taking a two-month family vacation. But we were the gas in his fuel line, and he was the turbo in our charger, and he was going to reward all of us with this summertime dream vacation.

From New York State to the West Coast, our home became a station wagon and a pop-up camper. National parks like Zion had us marveling at the beautiful and pristine caverns and nooks and crannies of carved-out earth. We were in awe of the bears as they walked like tourists among lined-up cars on the roads of Yellowstone. My siblings and I danced with indigenous people on their reservation, and we witnessed Old Faithful erupt with steam like an overheating radiator. Disneyland was the icing on the cake for us, especially for my sister Mary Ellen's thirteenth birthday. It was a dream come true. California's House of Mouse amusement park was unique at that time, and we experienced it firsthand. We then traveled north up the Pacific coast to visit cousins in Vancouver, Washington. This provided a brief respite from our living off-the-grid adventure. Mount Rainier seemed almost imaginary yet a majestic backdrop.

Every state we visited was the chance to write another postcard from the road and collect another sticker for the camper's door. By this time on the trip, dozens of postcards had been mailed, and that door that was once a blank canvas was filled with state stickers of all sizes, shapes, and colors, illustrating state mottos, mascots, and most memorable sites to see. It was a colorful collage of life-filled moments until it wasn't. I'd give just about anything to have that door as a souvenir to commemorate such an adventure.

My brother, Dave, refers to our escapade in Tijuana, Mexico, as if it was yesterday. He, like my dad, is a good storyteller. We were driving the desert highway and our station wagon quit. There we were, broken down, amid scraggy tumbleweeds and cascading mountains. Dad determined our quagmire was likely from bad gas received at the last rest area we stopped at before we crossed into Mexico. Someone had to walk back to the nearest town or hitch a ride with a complete stranger. I don't know whether mom and dad flipped a coin or played rock, paper, scissors, but the sight of watching mom walking away with a gas can in her hand and dust kicking up from her heels was like a scene from a western movie. You could almost hear the whistle from the theme song from *The Good, The Bad, and the Ugly.* And if you knew my mom, this was an odd role for her as she has always been the perpetual worrywart. But she demonstrated her true mama bear fashion that day.

A couple of hours later, and I'm sure many prayed rosaries, mom returned with a full gas can with the help of a road angel in a pickup truck. Dad filled up the station wagon and Tijuana was soon a distant memory.

Did I mention we were a Catholic family? We attended parochial elementary school, received the sacraments, and went to church on Sundays and holy days. We were running at full throttle with our faith. So, when we took vacations, God jumped in the car too. My parents always found a church for us on Sundays, which meant an overnight stay in a motel on Saturday nights while traveling. This would allow us to freshen up for Sunday Mass. Mom and dad always made sure there was a pool where we could have some fun and wash the vacation dirt off our skin.

With half the trip behind us and the West Coast in our rearview mirror, we were now eastward bound, back to reality. We made it as far as Denver on that Saturday. Usually, we would stay in a drive-in motel along Route 66. This Saturday, my parents took a detour and found a beautiful Italianate hotel called The Hotel Capri in downtown Denver. Ironically, the hotel was on the same block as the church, the convent, and the hospital with the country's renowned burn trauma unit. It certainly made it convenient to walk to church in the morning. Little did we know that the hospital would be where we found God in the early hours the next day. This location almost seemed predetermined.

The next morning, Sunday, July 27, we all began to take turns getting ready for church. We never made it. In a blink, our dream vacation turned into a nightmare from hell. No one could have predicted the tragedy that would unfold. My sister, Mary Ellen, who had just turned thirteen, was showering. She locked the bathroom door. I am sure she craved a bit of privacy from her eleven and nine-year-old brothers and her four-year-old baby sister, who loved being her shadow.

The screaming and chaos that ensued in that hotel room took years to erase. The water turned scalding hot while my sister was taking her shower. She couldn't turn the dials nor open the sliding glass door as the steam and heat had swollen the rubber casing. My dad tried to force down the locked door. He could not. My parents desperately tried to guide her from the other side of the impenetrable door. Every command or instruction was met with a roadblock. It was paralyzingly impossible. My brother Steve ran into the hallway and knocked on any hotel door that would answer. My brother came running back into our room with a man half-dazed and half-dressed from sleeping as it was early Sunday morning. This stranger tried to help my dad break down the door, but that too was an impossible feat.

After frantic calls to the front desk, the hotel manager ran into the room with his master keys; they wouldn't unlock the door. The situation grew more desperate. Suddenly Mary Ellen's screams stopped. This terrified us. Mom told my brothers and me to get by the bed and pray. The only way to reach Mary Ellen, now, was to take the hinges off the door and remove it from the door frame. It took many hands to do this agonizing task; more strangers showed up to help. Each hinge fell to the floor with a deafening thud. When the door was finally removed, the hot steam enveloped all of us like a shroud. Dad rushed through the foggy haze and found Mary Ellen unconscious at the end of the tub, blistering water still beating down on her. He scooped her out of the tub, cradled her in his arms, and delicately laid her fragile body on the ambulance stretcher waiting for her in our hotel room. Everyone watched in horror and disbelief.

I'll never forget the last image I had of my sister on that day. Her beautiful face writhed with such pain as from her neck down was raw and scalded. The medics then took Mary Ellen in an ambulance to that very hospital with the renowned burn trauma unit located on the same block as our hotel, that we noticed as we drove into Denver the day before. It was the last time I saw my sister alive. In fact, I never saw her again.

Our vacation of a lifetime was over. We were broken down in the darkness and we needed a divine tow truck.

Mom called her brother, Fr. Frank Taney, a Catholic priest and a Maryknoll missionary. While my parents steadfastly stayed by Mary Ellen's side in the hospital, Fr. Frank flew to Denver to be with us and hold prayerful vigil by my sister's bedside. He was supposed to be assigned to a parish in Seattle, and we were to visit him on this trip west, but shortly before we left for our vacation from our home in Waterloo, New York, he was reassigned to Buffalo, New York, so much closer to our home. Only God knew the reason for his transfer at the time. Fr. Frank would be needed more than ever by my family now.

News of my sister's devastating accident was heard throughout Denver later that morning. Strangers showed up to help; some to pray. Dave, Steve, and I were taken care of by nuns at the convent located by the church on the same block as the hotel and the hospital for the next three days so my parents and Fr. Frank could be with my sister. A special nun became a dear friend out of the storm that day and remained as such for the rest of her life. Sister Margaret Seton passed away many years ago, but on that fateful day, she came to our rescue and was instrumental in our moment of need.

During the next three agonizing days, Mary Ellen accepted her fate without complaint and, in the process, brought light to all who cared for her. Praying brought her peace. My uncle would pray the traditional Rosary (a series of devotional prayers to Mary and Jesus using prayer beads) with her. For ten beads, he would typically pray:

> *Hail Mary full of grace, the Lord is with you. Blessed are thou among women, and blessed is the fruit of thy womb, Jesus. Holy Mary, Mother of God, pray for us sinners now and at the hour of our death, Amen.*

But when he prayed a "new" version of that prayer with Mary Ellen, a version he was inspired to create using virtues in the place of "blessed" (a substitution of life-affirming qualities wished to manifest) she received an even greater peace, especially in her final moments.

The new prayer was this:

> *Hail Mary, full of* ***life****, the Lord is with* ***you****.* ***Peaceful*** *are you among women and* ***peaceful*** *is the fruit of* ***your*** *womb, Jesus. Holy Mary, Mother of God, pray for us to be* ***peaceful*** *now and at the hour of our death, Amen.*

I imagine the many virtues Fr. Frank used were *peaceful, loving, healing, protecting,* and *guiding. Peaceful* because of the great pain my sister had to endure. *Loving* because

Mary Ellen was such a loving human. *Healing* because while there was no hope for her recovery from third-degree burns over 90 percent of her body, my uncle and my sister were praying for us—her family—that we may heal from this pain. *Protecting* because we would need much. And finally, *guiding*, as "Momma Mary" would be taking Mary Ellen's hand and leading her to her new life with the Divine.

During my sister's last trial of life, her words were awe-inspiring: "We must right the wrongs in this life." Her empathy and compassion were older than her years. It was her constitution. Her intuition and trust in God were unwavering. She knew what was unfolding as she prepared for the launching of her soul when she said, "The gates to heaven are getting ready to open." To have been present in that moment was to have been part of something holy, of that I am certain.

Mary Ellen was many things: a *stellar* student, a *loving* sister, a *beautiful* daughter, a *loyal* friend, a *considerate* cousin, a *joyful* niece, and a *kind* human. And she always saw the best in others; she would rather take the hurt than cause it.

Three days passed. I don't remember who told us Mary Ellen died. Our vacation was over, and our lives were changed forever. Two of my parents' friends flew to Denver to drive our station wagon filled with scattered souvenir remnants and a pop-up camper with flannel sleeping bags, still smelling smoky from our last campfire, back to our home. A recently purchased Colorado state sticker would never find its place among the other stickers on the camper door. The six of us flew home, five in plane seats and one in a coffin. To say the rest is a blur is an understatement. Kids have a funny way of carrying on with business as usual. Maybe it is a mechanism to block out the pain or not inflict sadness upon our parents, but Dave, Steve, and I wanted to feel normal. We never did ever again.

My family felt a deep, gaping loss, yet we never talked of Mary Ellen's death until much later in our lives. Sister Margaret Seton told my parents that grief was like rust. It will slowly corrode the toughest metal. She encouraged talking about my sister's death. My parents tried many times, but as kids, we craved normalcy and avoided the subject. In 1969, post-traumatic stress disorder (PTSD) was real but wasn't a prolifically well-known acronym until years later. Grief counselors and therapists were not popular nor as available as today. And I suppose if we were trying to "act" normal, why force it? Why draw attention? It was easier to push through the pain silently or bury it deep inside.

We all managed our grief differently, and if you avoid your emotions or expose them to the elements, that rust will appear sooner or later. And if you don't take care of that rust, things break down and fall apart, like an old car.

Growing up, my parents proudly displayed school photos of my brothers and me on top of the piano. They would change year to year. Awful haircuts shifted to more modern and fashionable styles, crooked teeth were straightened by braces, and glasses were replaced with contact lenses. While the three of us morphed, my sister's seventh-grade photo, with her sweet smile

and the pretty pink dress my mom made for her, remained timeless on the wall. Dave, Steve, and I grew up and Mary Ellen stayed thirteen forever.

We never saw a picture of our family of six again. I imagine it was too painful for my parents to develop one roll of film from that family vacation. It wasn't until nearly forty years later that my parents thought it was time to open the box of memories and wounds, tuck the good ones in our pockets, and give the bad ones up to God. We gathered in my parents' living room and bore witness to a time we tried to forget. We saw photos of all of us having fun together, the family of six on the road trip of our lives before the oil oozed out and the engine seized.

I was four years old when Lala died. My nickname for her still rolls off my tongue as Mary Ellen sounds so formal to me even to this day. And yet, the very last memories of her etched into my mind were painful and tragic. I knew there had to be happier ones because throughout my life, I had snapshots in my head of "It's a Small World" at Disneyland, rolling around in the back end of the station wagon as my three siblings were tucked in the second row, driving through Idaho, Wyoming, and Montana. I remembered having our faces sketched in pencil by San Francisco street artists and how I could not believe we could make snowballs in the Rockies in July. But to see them come to life from the *click-click* of the slide projector that afternoon was so healing and validating. My internal memory card was hacked and on full display.

For me, this moment was cathartic as I suspect it was for all of us. I don't remember my life without grief. Trauma has a funny way of erasing memories. It was an epiphany for me that our cryptic past was real. This moment was a gift. These slides from our vacation of a lifetime presented the missing piece to a tragic and yet holy puzzle. At that moment my sister shifted from ghost to spirit in my world. It was transformational. I believe we all felt some rust flaking off us that afternoon. I miss my family of six but am grateful for our fab five.

My parents gave each of us a CD of photos from our 1969 California vacation for Christmas that year. I developed my favorite one and had it framed so my parents could again hang a picture of our family of six, a priceless piece of our family history.

The reaching-out-and-reaching-in effect is crucial, however—countless people connected with our family and comforted us during those early days of struggle. Often, solidarity with others is the real knowing and the gateway to healing. My parents used Mary Ellen's story to help guide and comfort other parents as they grieved the loss of a child. People have approached me throughout my life sharing how my parents' loss helped them with theirs. It's a reflex for me to share it when others grieve the loss of a child or the loss of sibling. I feel it is Lala's hands on my shoulders, guiding me in the right direction, and making connections with people I may have never met. From those have come deep and rich friendships I am blessed to have and may never have known if my life had been different.

Healing can take most of a lifetime. Maybe you get to a place where your grief is finally replaced with acceptance, or you know you will see your loved ones again. But until then, we will still celebrate Mary Ellen's birthday on July 16th and her "death-a-versary" (as a good friend calls it) on July 30th with remembrance Masses and a brunch with family and close friends. Later in the day, you can sometimes find my mom and me clinking glasses of bubbly and toasting to Mary Ellen's sweet life at her beautiful grave in the cemetery. There rests a statue of the Blessed Virgin Mary, as if she's taking watch of loved ones passed.

In 1969, Fr. Frank was divinely inspired to write *Mary Ellen's New Rosary for Young People*.[1] He was trying to motivate disenfranchised youth to reengage with the Rosary. Making it more relevant by adding a much-needed virtue seemed like an impossible possibility. With a shift it was transformed. It was published and circulated around the world and reprinted many times. That book told our family's story of loss and provided a guide to say the "new" Rosary, dedicated to my sister's memory. Her story and prayer are intermingled; one cannot exist without the other. Perhaps it wasn't just the Divine that inspired my uncle to put this prayer on paper but the person who loved it most, my sister. Therefore, I consider it our family's "Holy Grail," a tragedy yet a treasure of great personal, reflective, and spiritual significance to our lives. The tragedy is the loss. The treasure is healing, hope, and survival. While many believe God gives you what you can handle, I am more of a subscriber to: "the Divine helps you handle what you are given."

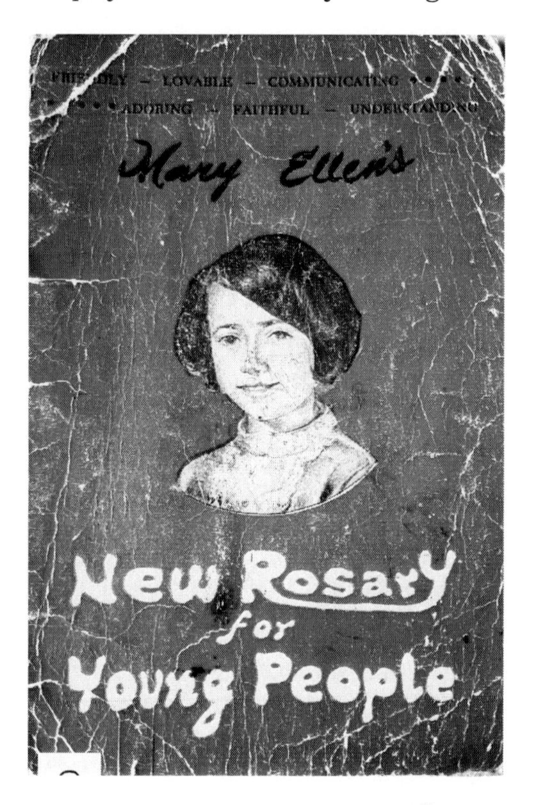


Grief is far and wide. You are never done with grief nor is grief done with you. It becomes part of you. How could it not? I think I have mourned Lala's loss more now as an adult and as a mother than when I was younger. Maybe it's the yearning of the sisterhood I missed. Maybe it's because I realize what gifts children are and the thought of losing one takes my breath away. Or maybe it's simply because I miss my sister. Missing, like grief, is lifelong. I feel so fortunate to have shared space with her as a child. It may be the holiest bond I will ever have in this life. She has always been my True North. I feel that my relationship with her has been fortified more through her death than her life. Her life had great meaning, but her death—like a vehicle identification number on a car; a unique code that follows the life of the vehicle—was purposefully, profoundly, and permanently woven throughout my life. My sister's death has not defined my life, but I am forever changed by it. Just because Lala is no longer with us in our earthly world doesn't mean she is gone forever. That is why talking about her and sharing her goodness keeps her alive. And energy never dies, that is proven. Ask any physicist. She is a vibration now. So her light still shines even if it's that low hanging star in the midnight blue of the night sky.

When someone asks me how my sister died, I always respond with "how much time do you have?" It's not a simple story to explain. Our loss is unique, but the magnitude of it is not. Parents will mourn their children. It's tragic and untimely. Families will grieve and meaning or purpose will need to be reconciled. Fr. Frank had a deep desire for his book, our story, her prayer to have a bigger, far-reaching effect. I believe I am divinely driving down this road for a reason and I hope *Holy Shift! Driving Through Grief in a Vintage VW* is that renewed purpose. Light does shine again after darkness. Hope is born from hopelessness. And faith will find anyone who is lost but still willing to be found.

# 2
# Pull The Emergency Brake

If "the family that prays together stays together," then we were the poster family. My parents' deep faith was instilled in us. In addition to going to church on Sundays, holy days, holidays, and remembrances days, we also prayed and meditated often upon Mary Ellen's Rosary.

Growing up, rosary beads were as prolific at our house as the cars we drove. Since my dad owned a dealership, the cars in our driveway changed all the time. He drove a different one home just about every week. My friends would call it my fleet. I never gave it a thought—it was the means to get from point A to point B. And like some of those revolving cars, each rosary strand at our house was significant. Some were like Dad's Buick Riviera with crushed velvet seats. Or the gold 1982 anniversary edition Pontiac Firebird that could seriously haul a$$. Others were more economical and basic. So as rosaries go, we had a fleet of them as well and they transported us spiritually down the divine highway.

It's a Catholic tradition when you die you are shown at your wake with rosary beads laced between your fingers. This symbolizes a manifestation of your faith. Or maybe it's a hope and a prayer for a fast pass to the pearly gates? Such things are typically removed from the deceased before the burial. So, we had many from our dearly departed hanging around our house. You could find them nestled in a colored carnival glass ashtray, clustered on the fireplace mantle, and even burrowed in the junk drawer. A strand always hung on my sister's timeless photograph on the wall with last Easter's palms. Even the Virgin Mary statue in the backyard had a strand of plastic rosary beads hanging from her outstretched hands.

My brothers and I received rosary beads for first holy communion and most likely every other sacrament we made. We had quite a trunk full at our access. Some were colored crystal, others were carved out of wood, and we even had some hand-blown from glass. Aunt Mabel's were silver plated, of course.

My favorite rosary beads were my sister's. My mom held them every time we prayed the Rosary together as a family. It wasn't a ritual until after my sister Mary Ellen died in 1969. On Sunday evenings before Marlin Perkins would air on *Wild Kingdom*, followed by Walt Disney, and eventually *All in the Family*—whereby I would often be sent off to bed because of the show's controversial topics—we would gather in the living room, light candles, and pray Mary Ellen's Rosary as a family. It was a weekly vigil.

Like an emergency brake in a car, the Rosary served as a layer of defense against our grief. Who knew fifty-nine beads, a miraculous medal, a cross, and a few word changes could help keep us from rolling backward on the hill? However, the Rosary we prayed together on Sunday nights sounded a little different than the one said by Mother Angelica on TV or Reverend Patrick Peyton, who led the Rosary rally crusades on the radio in the 1960s and '70s. The traditional is powerful and holy. But the Rosary we said was "full of life" and was pivotal in saving ours. The version we prayed had more horsepower than the classic. We injected more torque to the Hail Mary by adding mindful intention to each one. This helped my family shift forward and make the impossible, possible.

I remember being mesmerized by how the candlelight would dance off the blue crystals of my sister's rosary strand as my mom would thumb from bead to bead. Since there were five decades and five people in our family, we each had a turn to lead the prayer. I was always last, being the youngest, so I'd think about which virtues I needed for the week. Did I have a test? *Inspiring.* Was I having issues with friends? *Forgiveness.* Did I have a fight with my brothers? *Loving.* I always saved the last three beads in the decade for three specific virtues: *guiding, guarding*, and lastly, *protecting*. I always had a deep fear someone else would die in our family. It's hard not to develop an obsessive-compulsive disorder (OCD) of sorts, even in prayer. When I prayed these last three Hail Marys this way, each and every time, I felt more comforted and less fearful.

> *Hail Mary full of life the Lord is with you, protecting are you among women and protecting is the fruit of your womb, Jesus. Holy Mary, mother of God, pray for us to be protecting now and at the hour of our death, Amen.*

Now maybe my parents got more peace out of that half an hour than my brothers or I did at times, but if you do something long enough, it becomes a habit. Mindful praying proved to be a beneficial practice then and still is today. As each of us struggled to grieve, mourn, endure our disappointments, or celebrate happiness over the years, we always had Mary Ellen's Rosary to rely on to communicate with her. We couldn't call her on the phone or write her a letter, so meditating in prayer was the best way to feel her spirit and her presence; a connection.

Fr. Frank believed a few word changes could shift and transform a religious relic into a more purposeful prayer that the younger generation could be inspired by. Little did he know his divine intervention would also inspire a thirteen-year-old girl in her final days of life, creating an everlasting personal connection of love, loss, healing, and hope. And when they say faith can move mountains? It's true. My uncle was not only a Maryknoll missionary, but he was also a Hail Mary missionary, and his persistence convinced a church riddled with rigidity and tradition to welcome an opportunity for change. Alternative is a better word. For anyone interested in a more active way to pray the Rosary or the Hail Mary keep reading. This is not a replacement for the traditional version. This is simply a life affirming opportunity to engage in mindful prayer. It took some convincing. And it also took some getting used to, even for us. Change is progress. And you must progress through grief so why not give it a little more gas as you shift? Mary Ellen was the inspiration, Fr. Frank was the designer, and perhaps I am the promoter. Works for me.

# 3 The Spiritual Compass

It's been said that grief is a journey, not a destination. I have found that there is no checkered flag or finish line. It's a very long road and you will lose your way. Getting lost is easy. Getting found is not. You will undoubtedly drive down a one-way street or two in the wrong direction. You may drive in circles and end up exactly where you started. If you are mindful of the five stages of grief (denial, anger, bargaining, depression, and acceptance from the Kubler-Ross model),[2] frustration and weariness can also contribute to your road rage.

Direction is needed. But which way to go? If you've exhausted other options, maybe a spiritual compass can assist you on your journey. It can help to make the detours tolerable and the rough roads less uncomfortable. It's more dependable than GPS. It doesn't require Wi-Fi or the internet. The spiritual compass I am referring to is always available to you to help point you in the right direction. My family's spiritual compass was in Mary Ellen's Rosary. It was and is the Hail Mary that is full of life. And it helped us get on with ours.

When my sister died tragically and unexpectedly, faith, family, and friends served as our road crew. When we were low on gas, we fueled up with faith. When the car wouldn't start, we had family to give us a jump. When the check engine light came on, we had friends to assist with a road rescue. We were blessed to have all three. And sometimes even that wasn't enough. Not everyone is so lucky, and days can be dark going it alone. When life is out of control and you feel lost, faith can be your North Star. My family's faith in mindful praying of the Hail Mary helped to usher in the light, and fifty years later, the light still brightens. Think of it as driving with your high beams on—all the time. Oncoming traffic will flash you with their headlights as a hint to turn yours down; in this case, keep them shining brightly. Let them illuminate your path.

Now, I won't pretend believing in a higher power made it easy or that mindful praying took the pain away. But it helped navigate our path to peace. Trust me, there is no quick fix when you suffer loss and endure grief. Loving someone in *our* life means grieving them in *their* next. Sometimes it feels as if deep grief is the punishment of loving hard. But when you decide that the punishment is actually the privilege, that is when the light starts to come in. Healing from loss takes mindfulness. It takes time and work. It takes reaching out or someone reaching in. It requires being open to divine interventions and connections when they appear. It demands you shift through and experience the pain. If you don't sand the rust off your car before you use touchup paint, the paint will flake off and the rust will come back. Accepting loss doesn't mean you are okay or over it. You never are. It allows you to live with it, find meaning in it, and share it with others. The one thing humans have in common is loss. And we feel less alone when we know others ride along with us.

And just like your loss, your grief is unique to you. Often, we rely on others to help pull us out of the ditch. A divine tow truck will help get you back on the road. But this is your manifest. Others can't do the work for you. There is no cruise control. You must go at your speed. So be mindful of your speedometer. Going too fast is dangerous, and too slow can be problematic. If your spouse is managing the same grief as you, as in my parents' situation, you support each other, but you do, in fact, grieve differently and separately. You stay in your lane. One may dive into work projects. Another may find refuge in a volunteer effort to ease the pain. Drugs, alcohol, and addiction can be another's path. My dad had a dealership to operate every day, and my mom was raising the rest of us. It kept them both distracted and busy, and when it did not, the common thread between them was faith. And if losing Mary Ellen did not break their belief system—I am sure it bent it like the end of a dipstick—nothing could or ever would or ever did. My parents' faith in God, in each other, their marriage, their children, and their family and friends and most importantly the belief they would see their daughter again, was the key to their sustainability and the endless miles on their odometer. I will never know two stronger, more faithful and loving souls in my entire life. I am blessed to bear witness to such greatness on a level I can't comprehend. A true testament of what being "built to last" means—in this life and the next.

*Holy Shift!* is for you if you've lost a loved one. It is a legacy to my sister's life, death, and her lasting effect. It is for my uncle and the power of mindful prayer. It is for my dad, mom, brothers, and even for me. Our loss is now classified as old as an antique car—over forty-five-years old—but can be as fresh as yesterday. It is for my brother and sister-in-law, who feel the familiar pain my parents did after losing their son unexpectedly several years ago. It is for their oldest son, who must shift through his life without his brother and his best friend.

This book is also for my aunt who lost a son and to my cousins who lost their brother. They will always be relentless in their love for him. For another cousin who lost her sister to her husband's anger. For family friends who buried their dad next to their mom; as parents, they are eternally happy, but as children, you are left broken-hearted and sad. For a brave soul who recently lost her youngest son to an accident and her older son years before, leaving her no longer an earthly mom but a heavenly mother. May this book bring comfort and a knowing we walk different roads but still grieve together. For those who have had to be alone with their grief because of the COVID-19 pandemic, may this story and renewed prayer bring back hope.

I believe I am on this journey to cross paths with people who share the common denominator of losing a sibling. What evolves from our shared stories is a profound lifelong connection. I believe we've met because we needed each other; we are simpatico. You know who you are.

And then some souls come into your life serendipitously. Right place, right time? Maybe. I'm told it's a God wink. Your losses are devastatingly enormous: a husband, a father, a wife, a mother, even both parents.

The list of loved ones lost is never-ending. But what about those who have lost their faith in humanity or lost faith in themselves? The world can be the most unsettling place lately. This book is for you. Have you lost patience raising toddlers or teenagers? Take a moment. Do you feel lost in a marriage or a partnership? Maybe this will sustain you. Feeling lost in your job, with a friendship, a situation, or with yourself? Find hope here.

Inexcusable, unacceptable, and unforgivable things happen to all of us. We are all connected in loss and grief. This book is for anyone lost in a lifetime or a moment and looking to be found or needing help getting back on the road. Grief can settle into your bones and drive you inward. And you can't be found if you don't send a distress signal. So don't be afraid to turn on your flashers or honk your horn. A Hail Mary moment may be the road rescue you require.

> *Hail Mary full of life the Lord is with you. Helpful are you among women and helpful is the fruit of your womb, Jesus. Holy Mary, mother of God, pray for us to be helpful now and at the hour of our death, Amen.*

Do you see how asking for help can also make you helpful toward others? It's like a hybrid vehicle that uses gas and electric working together to power the engine. Dual purposed. So power up.

# 4 The Divine Tow Truck

When Fr. Frank's letters arrived *par avion* there was always a thrill ready to jump out of the white envelope framed with red and blue stripes indicating a letter had flown around the world to our mailbox. He always had something exciting to share and it always finished with his less than legible signature and his trademark "happy angel scribble."

Perhaps he was heaven-sent. His wings were moving so fast all the time that we could never see them. But we could feel them. And my family did more than ever during our loss. Fr. Frank was the divine tow truck we needed. His unexpected relocation to Buffalo allowed him to spend a lot of time with my family after my sister died. He provided unconditional spiritual support and comfort as we navigated through the early stages of grief. I know he provided great counsel to my parents.

"Long live freedom" is something my uncle Fr. Frank Taney said much and often. He appreciated and respected—even if he didn't agree with—someone's view, position, or status; he believed they were free to subscribe to it. He was the center of family gatherings, always a house full of Irish-loving folk with some French mixed in. Fr. Frank loved to set the stage, interject a delicate subject, and magically disappear while everyone discussed, deliberated, or debated the topic.

Fr. Frank was a better driver than a passenger. He liked to be in charge, behind the wheel, but never took credit, even if it was due. If it wasn't for his belief in revitalizing the Rosary, our path to peace might have been different or even unattainable. Because he was a Maryknoll Missionary priest, he spent a good portion of his calling in the Philippines. He was always surrounded by loving people amid the dangerous unrest in Davao City or when his church burned to the ground. We worried about his safety, but he had a rebel spirit, a revolutionary heart, and was a dedicated soldier for his faith. The Virgin Mary was his "Momma Mary" and he referred to her as such much and often. He had an amazing devotion to her all his life. And when my brothers and I and our cousins heard the news that he was coming home on furlough? If it was Christmastime, well, counting down the days to his arrival superseded the advent calendar, sorry Jesus. Fr. Frank coming home was like anticipating Santa!

And if he visited in the summer, no kid complained about going to church because he held Mass outside in nature. He always made the scripture readings relevant to anyone in attendance. And there was always a job for every niece or nephew, even if only boys served the altar back then. Everyone was included. I remember sitting as a young girl on a chair next to Fr. Frank, and you would have thought I won the lottery. When I attended Catholic school, girls were not allowed to altar serve. But during the summer, Fr. Frank broke the rules, and well, the church was in our backyard and the Vatican police were over four thousand miles away, so no one was coming to put me in altar-serving jail.

My dad would always take a car off the dealership lot so that Fr. Frank could have his "wheels" when he came home. He always had people to see, places to go, and good deeds to do. As kids, we would ride with him in his car to go to the grocery store or to visit Aunt Mabel, and he would look back at us kids in the back seat and say, "Look! No hands!" We would squeal with delight because we believed angels were driving the car.

We could not see over the seat to realize that his knees were steering the wheel.

My uncle was good-natured, the life of the party, but a religious and devout priest. He was open-minded to a point whereby he could see a situation through many lenses, but to his core, God was first. He left wiggle room for his family, however. He never pressured my Episcopalian husband to become Catholic. Fr. Frank always respected the choices of others, even when it came to religion. But that didn't stop him from asking my husband to be an altar server at home Masses, though. Everyone was always welcome to come to the table.

After we were married, Fr. Frank came to our house to bless it. It felt more like an exorcism as each room was blessed with holy water and a Hail Mary. Our bedroom was no exception, as he knew how much we wanted children. When we were dealing with infertility, my husband and I eventually chose the path of in vitro fertilization (IVF) to become pregnant. Fr. Frank said to me, "That is why God created scientists."

One of Fr. Frank's last gifts that he gave us before he died was baptizing our twins in November 2001. Because the babies were preemies, the baptismal Mass was held at my parents' house. We believed, as Fr. Frank did that day, that God was everywhere. Everyone felt it. Fr. Frank left the next day to drive back to Florida, where he died days later. His enlarged heart had given enough.

They say when an older person dies, a baby is born to take their place. Maybe that is why God sent a set of twins. If that is true, then we are more than doubly blessed. However, missing him every day is an understatement. But his crowning achievement was being inspired to create a more relevant version of the Rosary, a "repurposed" version, changing the Hail Mary with a little shift. He wondered if a bit of bodywork to an old classic would catch on.

As my sister was dying that fateful summer in a Colorado burn unit, he was there with her in her final days. He witnessed the incredible peace she received from praying this rejuvenated version. The transformation of hospital nurses and doctors who cared for Mary Ellen solidified the power of this prayer. I don't think Fr. Frank could know the effect it would have going forward in our lives and countless others. My sister died from her injuries but not before her time affected those around her. *Mary Ellen's New Rosary For Young People* was certainly new at the time and for young people, but it has such life-affirming qualities that I often call it Mary Ellen's Living Rosary For All People. This mindful praying of the Rosary is for everyone.

And if you are wondering, it caught on.

*Second Gear:*

# Back On The Road

# 5 Time For Tune-Up

When you are grieving the loss of a loved one or a situation, it takes a trunk full of tools to get you back on the road. Maybe you have found the perfect balance. Good for you and keep going. Please share your experience with me at: michelle.lebrun315@gmail.com.

If you are struggling and think you may want to try and incorporate the Hail Mary full of life into your life, your healing regimen, your morning ritual, your evening prayer, your yoga meditation, or a Hail Mary moment as I often refer to frustrations on any given day, give it a try.

Think of Mary Ellen's Rosary as a living version. The Hail Mary is the star, and with each prayer bead, you insert a virtue like *peaceful, loving,* or *kind*. There is a list of virtues on pages 58–59 that could apply to your life in that moment of prayer. Instead of repeating prayer after prayer this version allows you to make each Hail Mary new and adaptable to your moment. Whether you have thirty minutes to pray the entire rosary or ten seconds to say a mindful Hail Mary, peace comes. But you must practice. It is an intentional connection with the Divine, and it requires exercise.

The sport of car racing requires more than a competitor with a passion for driving fast on a track. They train. Mindful praying is the same. The driver needs to be an active participant. The driver needs to be "all in" and engaged. This Hail Mary is a crossover prayer. You need not be Catholic to say it; it transcends religious boundaries. It is designed to fit everyone's spiritual-ability level and provides abundant opportunity to strengthen and fortify your relationship with the Divine. This Hail Mary is also like a cross trainer prayer because it not only provides devotional exercise for your mind but spiritual nutrition for your soul. Who knew a shift could have the powerful intention to help you find your direction, center, balance, or focus?

But to be entirely effective, this prayer allows you to take an inventory of what you need more of in your life, how you want to live, or what you need to procure for another person.

Is it time for a spiritual tune-up? Has someone hurt your feelings? Have you hurt another's? Then pray for forgiveness:

> *Hail Mary full of life, the Lord is with you. Forgiving are you among women, and forgiving is the fruit of your womb, Jesus. Holy Mary Mother of God, pray for us to be forgiving now and at the hour of our death, Amen.*

Do you need to be more present for others? Pray for compassion:

*Hail Mary full of life, the Lord is with you. Compassionate are you among women and compassionate is the fruit of your womb, Jesus. Holy Mary Mother of God, pray for us to be compassionate now and at the hour of our death, Amen.*

Do you have a loved one that is ill? Pray for healing:

*Hail Mary, full of life, the Lord is with you. Healing are you among women, and healing is the fruit of your womb, Jesus. Holy Mary Mother of God, pray for us to be healing now and at the hour of our death, Amen.*

Do you have teenagers? Pray for patience:

*Hail Mary full of life, the Lord is with you. Patient are you among women, and patient is the fruit of your womb, Jesus. Holy Mary Mother of God, pray for us to be patient now and at the hour of our death, Amen.*

What do you need? Plug it in and pray.

Prayers with beads have been incorporated into many religions for centuries. Whatever your religion or belief, a little intention and meditation on virtues are amazingly powerful. This prayer brought light back into our family and got us back on the road. May you seek a peaceful understanding of your struggles, be grateful for your blessings, and hope that all things are possible through the Divine. The answers you seek may not be the answers you get. My family prayed to save Mary Ellen. Instead, we were asked to shift. And while we are reminded daily of her absence, we are fueled just as much with carrying on and going forward. All things light and right.

# 6 Classic Curb Appeal

Do you know how to become timeless, relevant, and hip among fans? You need curb appeal and pray it doesn't fade. Give yourself a nickname, a slogan, or an acronym. The Blessed Virgin Mary and the Volkswagen (VW) have much in common. They were created and chosen for a purpose—to make a difference in people's lives. I am a fan of both. I have a spiritual devotion to Mary and a love affair with my 1967 VW Bug, "Sweet Pea."

Turns out, this VW—the Beetle, the Bug, the Lady Bug, or the Flea—became adored worldwide as an iconic symbol of peace and love that has been seen parked at church, at music festivals, and at the beach. The Blessed Virgin Mary, like the Bug, is accessible to all, continues to bring joy, and is loved the world over. Her "vehicle," however, was birthing her son, Jesus. While my Bug, Sweet Pea, is special, she could never birth a Savior, but she definitely gives rise to the corners of peoples' mouths as she beep beeps down the road.

Mary also goes by many names. Some call her the Virgin Mary, the Holy Mother, the Queen of Peace, Momma Mary, the Mystical Rose, and Star of the Sea. To me, she is and always will be "the BVM"—the Blessed Virgin Mary. In my life she is all things classic, timeless, relevant, and always in style.

My devotion to her began back in my childhood. I was recovering from my sister's loss; she and my sister shared the same name, so maybe I was devoted to both. But each May was Mary's month. I'd have a grotto of sorts in my bedroom with Mary's statue and a small vase of spring flowers, being mindful of both Marys in my life. In grammar school, I was chosen to be "Queen of the May" and crown Mary with flowers in a special prayer service. Somehow, I was often picked to play the role of the Virgin Mary at the Christmas school pageant, too. Maybe that was a sign I needed to be more devout. An honor, nonetheless. As an adult, I am even more in awe of her strength and courage to affect positive change in the world.

So here is what "the BVM" means to me.

### *The Mother of all Mechanics*

When you find a good car mechanic you are not only thankful, but you keep going back. Why? Because they are skilled at their craft, they have a great reputation, they know your car inside and out, and they are reliable. They get your car working and get you back on the road. You trust them. Sounds just like most moms, doesn't it? I would dare to say the same is true with the BVM. In the big picture, she is mom of all. In fact, I'd give her the title of the "mother of all mechanics." She is always there, she is trustworthy, she's dependable, and she knows you better than you know yourself. Taking time to have a divine connection with her will undoubtedly get you back on the road. It is a two-way street, however. Don't expect something for nothing. You must give to get. What Momma Mary requires doesn't cost a thing. She only asks for your heart and your ability to engage in her prayer, the Hail Mary. Whether it is the traditional or the Hail Mary full of life version, talk to your momma, give your worries over to her. She is the grand fixer as she gives you the strength to make change, to shift, to move forward. I know this to be true. I am not capable of shifting through life without a good mechanic. Are you?

## *The SUV Of The Spirit Highway*

When looking at the BVM's life, she has been known to handle any terrain—even the roughest—with grace. I would say she is a religious crossover, like an SUV. She has endured and is durable through the centuries. She is versatile and spiritually fueled on gas, electric, and diesel. And she's not just for Catholics, as some people like to think. She is present in the Christian Bible and also important in Islam. In fact, she is the only woman to have a chapter (surah) named for her in the Quran[3]. She is the spiritual Queen of Peace, and people worldwide have prayed to her for that. Peace for many things. The list is long, but if we start with a loving and accepting heart and consideration for our differences, then maybe a unifying prayer can heal. If the same prayer can help people who have suffered loss, as my family, then the power vested in it is providential.

And speaking of unifying, when it comes to religion, we are probably more similar than we realize. Religion, although divinely inspired, is like a car. There are many makes, models, and sizes. Now think of prayer as energy for the car. Prayer is action, and without energy, cars don't work. Now think of faith as the road, our belief system that is universal and unique at the same time. We all drive our cars filled with specific fuel or energy on the same road that will eventually lead us to the one higher power. I think we will all get a good laugh that we spent time, money, and care to be buried in religiously divided cemeteries only to find out we all eventually ended up in the same place. A place finally full of love, understanding, and appreciation for all. It won't matter what car we drove.

### *Timeless Classic*

The "Flying Lady" adorns and emanates the Rolls Royce mythos. No doubt the forward-leaning woman with billowing clothes like an angel is the most iconic hood ornament of all time. Some would say owning a Rolls is a religious experience. I will never know. But while I am referring to timeless class, undeniable beauty, and staying power, what I do know is that the BVM's ethos radiates enlightenment and influence that is centuries old. Her beauty is radiantly brilliant and her power to affect transcends. She, too, is iconic, and adored worldwide. Miraculous medals, necklaces, scapulars, and prayer beads are created in her likeness and are used for meditation and prayer. I have several necklaces I enjoy wearing and feel fortified when I do. The BVM is also the cornerstone of any grotto. "Mary on the Half Shell" guards many a backyard or garden worldwide. Growing up, my dad built a monument to her in our pool patio. She was in the "half shell" as kids joked, but she was built upon a beautiful rock garden and shined brightly every night. Now that my parents have moved, she did too, and watches guard over my mom's yard, a reminder of her constancy.

## Hail Mary Pass

It's easy to understand why some consider the BVM as the "go to" in times of hopeless possibility. Because the Hail Mary is a devotion prayed to her, circumstances often rely and depend on the Hail Mary to defy odds, address hopeless situations, or change plans during desperate moments. It's referred to as the "Hail Mary pass," and venues from football to politics have tossed it around hopeful for success in times of great need. When it works in football, the impossible becomes possible. It's a miracle.

When it doesn't work out quite as we would like I refer to my onion theory. The miracle hides inside the heart of the onion. It takes some peeling back of the layers to find the meaning. There have been politicians desperate for a Hail Mary pass, and when all of Mary's Hail couldn't produce a desirable outcome, such as winning a presidential bid or a second term, maybe she had other plans—my onion theory. There is the obvious and the not-so-obvious power to the Hail Mary, no doubt, but as the Rolling Stones sang, "You can't always get what you want...but you get what you need."[4]

## The Original Social Influencer

Imagine if we took a page from the BVM's playbook when it came to social media. Perhaps she is the original "social influencer." If we looked at how she lived her life and applied her social platform to our daily living, might our lives be consumed with more of an *uplifting, peaceful, loving, supporting,* and *compassionate* lifestyle? Could taking cues from her create a more inspiring, positive, and kinder virtual reality, especially for our kids? The BVM's virtuous life was her birthright, *modus operandi* (MO), and legacy. Who would not want to emulate her moral code?

For instance, she was born without original sin; we were. God was certainly preparing her for something special. Then the angel Gabriel proclaimed that she, a young teenager, would give birth to the Christ child. The doubt cast upon her by others had to be tremendous. Yet she was *faithful, loyal,* and *trusting* with God's plan. Giving birth to Jesus and being his mother makes the BVM the most revered woman of the Church. This is a testament to how *courageous, hopeful,* and *loving* she was throughout her life. At the moment of her son's crucifixion, she had to have been *sorrowful* and *suffering* on the inside, but she was *adoring, prayerful,* and *mournful* on the outside, once again, *accepting* God's plan. No doubt much was asked of her during her life. She didn't question and she didn't quit.

### *The Leading Lady*

And the Academy Award goes to—the star of the Rosary—otherwise known as the Hail Mary. As the mother of Jesus, she bore witness to the joyful, sorrowful, glorious, and luminous mysteries and moments of her son's life while maintaining her virtuous MO. What a lifetime role as the leading lady! May moms everywhere be so inspired. And as a mom, experiencing all the moments of my kids' lives, I know my virtues haven't always been intact. That is why I pray to the BVM and why I meditate on her virtues and ask for a refill or a tune-up often.

## Kicked In The Stained-Glass Ceiling

I am inspired all the time by amazingly courageous women who pave the way for others. Ponder this: the BVM not only broke through, but she kicked in the proverbial stained-glass ceiling. What role is bigger, more crucial, or more revered than to be Jesus's mother? She was the CEO, the driving force behind Jesus (as mothers are for their children), and Jesus was the COO; he made sure "the work" was carried out according to God's plan. I am not challenging one's importance over the other here with hierarchical acronyms. However, without Mary, there would be no Jesus. Contemplate that.

The BVM was also the producer of her prayer. Sometimes if you want something done, do it yourself once and then delegate. It has been said by Christian folklore that she appeared to St. Dominic in the thirteenth century, gave him rosary beads, and inspired him to promote it. What other woman in religious history has a string of beads with meditative devotional prayers prayed by faithful believers worldwide in her honor? The BVM is not only the cornerstone of the traditional Rosary, but she is also the spiritual compass in my sister Mary Ellen's Rosary. This prayer will be prayed until the end of time. This prayer will continue to provide peace to all who pray it. That is powerful.

The BVM has that classic curb appeal that is timeless and transcends. What the Hail, Mary?!

My family's lives changed dramatically on Sunday, July 27, 1969. We did not get what we wanted from that day, but we got what we needed. Perhaps we got the Hail Mary pass of a lifetime to be able to endure my sister's loss, making the impossible, possible. My onion theory? Well, we certainly spent years peeling back the layers of our loss until we found the heart of that stinkin' onion. The bitter was finally replaced with sweet.

My mother believes—as many others do—that the Blessed Virgin Mary and the Rosary (old or new) and the power of the Hail Mary will save the world. I certainly believe getting more people engaged in virtuous prayer is good. Maybe we need to be the link in the drivechain versus the kink. Being mindful of our virtuosities or where we come up short could be providential and the change the world needs.

# 7

# From The Model A Ford To The Mustang

Catholics have had a devotion to Mary and her Rosary for over seven hundred years. In fact, bead praying is more universal than people know. Orthodox Christianity, Islam, Hinduism, and Buddhism religions pray with beads. Beads are used to count or keep track of prayers or devotions. Some people find meditative, protective, and relaxing properties from bead praying. Perhaps my "Rosary for Dummies" would go like this: it is a series of mother-son vignettes meditated in prayer. The strand has fifty-nine beads, and each bead is a prayer. Mary is the centerpiece as she has fifty-three Hail Mary beads. Each bead is an opportunity for Mary to intercede to Jesus on your behalf.

Consider Mary the old-fashioned telephone operator and she is connecting you to the person on the other end of the phone, Jesus. All things go through Mary to get to Jesus. Each time you say the Rosary, you focus on the seasons of Jesus's life. They are called the mysteries. As in life, there are four seasons to his life: the joyful, the sorrowful, the glorious, and the luminous. They are foundational to the Rosary because they describe how Jesus lived, loved, suffered, and was redeemed.

Think of them as the road map each time you pray the Rosary or say a mindful Hail Mary. As his mother, Mary witnessed all of it, and perhaps as any mom would, she felt it all more deeply than perhaps even he did, at times. As a mother, I know that I often felt more affected when my kids were hurt or upset than they did. When your child goes through something uncomfortable, you want to take care of it, but if you do, they never learn to take care of things themselves. Mama Bear is sometimes difficult to control when you need to guide from the side. In essence, we pray to Mary while experiencing moments of Jesus's life. It's a prayerful story.

It is predictable and powerful. And if it works for you, keep on.

Unlike most traditional prayers, automobile technology is constantly changing. The design of new models takes something old and makes it better: more power, better fuel efficiency, more options. Ford's Model A paved the way for the Mustang. So why not change a traditional prayer? That's what my uncle, Fr. Frank, did when he was inspired to create *Mary Ellen's New Rosary for Young People* in 1969.

As mentioned previously, the difference is the shift in the Hail Mary. By adding a virtue, it becomes a more personal and a more powerful prayer. It is full of life for your life. Now instead of simply reciting a memorized prayer to Mary, you are looking at your life at that moment and asking Mary for something. It requires you to be an active participant in prayer versus passive repetition. It makes you think about what one of her virtues you need in that moment or throughout your life. What do you need more of? In other words, what bead do you need?

Did you lose a loved one like my family? Ask to be more *accepting*. Have you lost your temper in a traffic jam or with your teenagers? Ask to be more *patient*. Have you lost a friendship because of a misunderstanding? Ask for *understanding*. Have you lost your respect for something someone did to you? Ask to be *forgiving*. Have you lost your sensitivity toward others? Ask to be more *compassionate*. Have you lost yourself in worry about your grown children? Ask for Mary's mothering *protecting* virtue. Feeling lost in your job? Ask to be *renewed* or *rejuvenated* or *helpful* to find a new one. Feeling like you have lost your way, your path, your direction? Ask Mary to be more *guiding*. Feeling lost or anxious in your mental, emotional, or physical stability? Ask to be *strengthened* or more *resilient* and *to protect* your mind, heart, and body.

With a few word changes, old becomes new again.

> *Hail Mary, full of life, the Lord is with you. Healing are you among women and healing is the fruit of your womb, Jesus. Holy Mary Mother of God, pray for us to be healing now and at the hour of our death, Amen.*

It is mindful. It is purposeful. It is renewed every time. It has an engaging energy that gives power to the participant. And for those that pray my sister's version, take note that I have removed the word "sinners" from the response. This is author's choice with a divine wink. I realized somewhere along my life and growing up with this Hail Mary I never said "sinners" anyway. Maybe it felt too fire and brimstone. And let's be honest, we are born sinners. We mess up, screw up, and let people down every day. Let's focus less on what we are and concentrate more on what we can be. Hail Mary!

As I moved through my life, my sister's Rosary has become purposeful to me, no doubt. But I also found that simply praying the mindful Hail Mary full of life can change the trajectory of any given moment. It can elevate your concentration, clarity, and comfort. Sometimes we only have a moment, and that is okay. It's a spiritual sprint. I believe that any prayer is a good prayer. The result is a connection. If you have more time, pray the entire Rosary. Some people say it several times a day. Whether it is a moment or a marathon, you must get your permit before your driver's license. Just get behind the wheel.

Having trouble? Suggested virtues like *loving, patient,* and *kind* are on the following pages. But if you take a moment and meditate on "living more like Mary and loving more like Jesus," it could be the key to achieving peace and harmony in your life. The best thing about this Hail Mary? It is personal to you. It's like buying a car. What make, model, or style do you need? You can design it to fit your lifestyle.

We are needy. Mary is here to help. And you must understand that because we pray to the Divine doesn't always give us the results we desire. We prayed for a miracle that my sister would survive. The miracle was that we survived her death. Often, we get what we need, not what we want. Praying for one or many of Mary's virtues is one thing, that's the easy part. A fake-it-till-you-make-it approach will only take you so far. The hard part is believing and mindfully injecting them into your life. So, start with one bead. Like anything, it takes practice, and if you don't engage, you will only get what you give. It's a spiritual investment. And much like a car, if you don't bring it to the mechanic for regular maintenance or repairs, it will give you only so many miles. So, make the investment and enjoy the shift.

# 8 Under The Hood

Essentially all prayer is the spiritual act of connecting with the Divine. The Hail Mary full of life is a virtuous and intentional way of praying that can resonate with *all* people of *all* faiths and perhaps more meaningful to those without any.

When you pop the hood of your car and look at all the parts, they are all essential to a perfectly tuned automobile. Remove one and the engine doesn't run or doesn't run well. Everyone struggles, has doubts, endures pain, experiences loss. These affect our well-being. As humans, we all need hope, crave joy, want answers, pray for miracles, desire understanding, believe in harmony, require tolerance, and hope for peace. The virtues manifested through a Hail Mary moment, or a marathon, are many. There is a bead for every need. This is how we gain over any loss; this is how we keep moving forward. The following are some of my favorite Hail Mary virtues that can be used in this prayer.

### *Loving*

Not everyone is loving these days. But you can only control yourself, right? So, do you need to be more loving? Do you desire a more loving relationship with your spouse, partner, child, sibling, parent, or friend? Then pray for it. Often, by manifesting loving, you are likely to achieve it. Be open and be ready.

### *Forgiving*

*This* is a big intention. But before we start manifesting it for others, try starting with ourselves. Forgiveness is powerful. Have you done wrong to another person? Pray for yourself. Has someone wronged you? Pray for them! It's kind of like when you are on a plane and the captain says put your mask on before you assist others. If you have lost oxygen, you can't help others now, can you? Same thing with forgiveness. We are not perfect beings. We do wrong things every day. So start by forgiving yourself first, then forgive others. Harboring anger toward another only hurts you. Try the freedom of forgiveness, it's not only liberating it is empowering.

### *Kind*

Why would there be a plethora of best-selling books on being kind if they weren't integral to the survival of humanity? Being kind starts with me. Being kind starts with you. Like a stone tossed into the lake, the ripples will turn into waves and eventually reach the other side having an effect.

### *Patient*

Patience is in short supply toward others. Whether you are a parent raising kids, having a misunderstanding with your partner, feeling completely frustrated at work, or stuck in traffic and you feel the road rage coming over you, being more patient is warranted for everyone and serves as a great diffuser of anger. Patience goes hand in hand with tolerance. The events of the world have us all a little less tolerant. Pray for patience and be mindful of your tolerance with others. A little of both goes a long way.

### *Courageous*

Maybe you resemble this virtue or require more to face a problem, an issue, a challenge, or a relationship. Maybe you need the courage to try something new. Take that step to make a decision that will be life changing. Maybe you are requiring courage to live with integrity or more authentically or require courage to live your truth. Perhaps you need a more virtuous path to walk. Or to say no to a demand or yes to a request. We all can be courageous, and it often starts with one moment, one action, one intention.

### *Compassionate*

Are you? Do you feel for others? Do you walk their path? Can you imagine walking their path? The key is feeling their path. We all experience times where compassionate consideration for another is desperately needed, whether we are the givers or receivers. It is usually innately grounded, but if it's not in you or you are feeling depleted, maybe this bead is for you.

### *Healing*

Everyone is struggling with something where a thought or prayer of healing will help. Physical, mental, emotional, spiritual, or financial ill-health is far affecting. Cancer? Depression?

Anxiety? Running low to empty on faith? Too much money gets you a better view but can run amok. Not enough can cause despair, hunger, or homelessness. No one or situation is perfect. More healing can be the bead you need.

### *Protecting*

As a young child that experienced trauma, protecting was one bead I was constantly focused on. When you suffer loss at a young age and you don't quite understand it, it can haunt you. You can worry and obsess about losing someone else.

As a parent, I have always prayed for protection for my kids, and I always will. It's the Hail Mary we say as a family before we start any trip. It's the Hail Mary I pray in the air when flying at takeoff or landing or during turbulence. It's the Hail Mary I pray late at night when I worry about my kids at college. It's the Hail Mary I pray when my mom doesn't answer her phone. It's the Hail Mary I pray over and over at night when I can't sleep. It's the Hail Mary I pray when my gut tells me to think otherwise. It's masked as worry, and worry is wasted energy. Yep. This bead is particularly an overworked one for me.

### *Peaceful*

Well, everyone should be manifesting peace for harmony in our crazy world. But maybe there is unrest in your community. Perhaps there is a disagreement between you and your neighbor, family, or in-laws. Maybe it's a miscommunication. Leading with a peaceful heart will always lessen tension. We may not always get the result we desire, but at least we know our hearts are pure with a peaceful intention to achieve harmony. Make love, not war, begins with peace. Let it begin with me.

### *Hopeful*

Don't feel it? Feeling small in a big world? Overwhelmed with hopelessness? Often it is not as easy as removing "less" and adding "ful" to "hope." People have real issues with hope. It's easy to see why. We need reasons to feel hopeful again. Families are separated at borders. People are discriminated against. Lack of tolerance to our differences. Children are hungry. Homelessness is rampant. Mental health is in crisis. Joblessness is ever present. War is easier to engage in than achieving peace within families, across borders, and with faraway countries. When did we become a people of no hope? We must do our part to instill hope in others in whatever small or large way that we can. It is infectious and will spread. It is our way back to the center.

### *Joyful*

Big things don't always have to happen to make you feel joyful. Often, it's the smallness of moments that yield the most joy. It's easy to overlook small joy because we have come to expect big joy to bulldoze us over. Take a walk. Pick a bright yellow dandelion; let it brighten your moment. Then pick a dandelion that bloomed and prepared to seed among the field. Don't you remember the joy you felt as a child blowing those feathery tendrils into the air and watching them float endlessly like wishes into the wind? Don't worry; spring is coming.

### *Thankful*

The *Oxford English Dictionary* defines thankful as a feeling. Each one of us has something to feel thankful for, whether it's food on your table, a roof over your head, an education, a loving and supportive family, loyal friends, safe travels, employment, good health, your faith, or that you got to see another sunrise. Being thankful for feeling the small things, obvious and basic things, is where the magic is.

### *Grateful*

Being grateful is defined as an action. Take your thankful feelings and put them into grateful action. Walking the talk, as they say.

### *Understanding*

*This is big. Really big*. Especially in today's divided and conflicted world. Please pray for understanding. We all have opinions, thoughts, and ideas. We do not share the same belief system. We may never agree. And our opinions are our own. Appreciating and respecting the opinions of others is even harder when divisiveness is ruling the conversations these days. Most of the problem is misunderstanding; pray for an understanding of the misunderstanding and more living like Mary and loving like Jesus here.

### *Accepting*

We are all born with our own DNA, therefore, we are uniquely unique. Appreciate the similarities we share and accept the differences that define our truths. If we are living our truth, our differences should not matter.

Here is a list of suggested virtues you can use. Don't be limited by what you don't see here. Insert what you wish to manifest.

*Assuring, attentive, achieving, adaptable, admirable, adoring, affirming, artistic, advising, authentic, affectionate, approachable, appreciative, brave, believing, beloved, caring, courageous, cheerful, compassionate, consistent, contemplative, courteous, creative, cooperative, calm, committed, confident, constant, comforting, charismatic, concerned, dignified, decisive, dedicated, divine, devout, dauntless, diligent, earnest, encouraging, enthusiastic, enduring, enlightening, energetic, extraordinary, friendly, forgiving, faithful, gracious, grateful, gentle, genuine, generous, guarding, guiding, happy, heroic, harmonious, hopeful, humble, helpful, humorous, heavenly, hospitable, holy, honest, innocent, intrepid, inspiring, initiating, involved, intelligent, idealistic, interested, just, joyful, jubilant, kind, loving, lovable, listening, loyal, meditating, modest, mediating, meek, mature, merciful, obliging, offering, outstanding, observing, protecting, preparing, providing, pure, prudent, peaceful, patient, prayerful, persevering, praising, resolute, radiant, refreshing, renewing, rejoicing, respectful, relaxed, reasonable, responsible, realistic, reverent, redeeming, sincere, strengthening, serene, silent, sympathetic, spiritual, serving, studious, sensitive, strong, tactful, teaching, thankful, thoughtful, tolerant, trusting, trustworthy, transcending, truthful, unprejudiced, uniting, unfailing, uncomplaining, unpretentious, universal, understanding, victorious, virtuous, watchful, wise, zealous.*

If the Rosary is not your thing, maybe the Hail Mary full of life is. And if this Hail Mary doesn't universally apply to you for whatever belief or reason, maybe a more virtuous-filled life does. Often, we don't know what we need until we are behind the wheel. Go ahead and take her for a spin.

# 9 Always Have A Spare Tire

Not everyone is good with change. I know I am not. But this version of the Hail Mary has been a part of my life for fifty-three years. It's my go to meditative prayer for the big things—and the small. I like to call them Hail Mary moments: whether it was the impetus for writing this book or someone cutting me off in traffic and flipping *me* off, or my dog chewing my favorite flip-flops for the second pair. Trust me when I tell you: it can help you find your center. And when you get a flat tire, you will be thankful you had a spare. Driving without one only to discover you don't have one when you need it—well, you might want to reconsider. Having some spiritual backup could provide relief to your grief. But I know what you are thinking.

*I'm not Catholic.*

You don't have to be. In fact, I prefer you weren't. I challenge you to see for yourself the power in this prayer. It doesn't belong to Catholics; it belongs to everyone. Besides, the non-ecclesiastical English version of Catholic means universal, all embracing, and inclusive. It matters not what your religion is but what's in your heart. One doctor who was caring for my sister in the hospital before she died was a nonbeliever. After spending time in her room and being that close to a beautiful soul, who found such peace in this Hail Mary, he was converted and became a believer in its power.

### *I don't believe in God.*

Many people don't, but perhaps you have faith in a divine being. Maybe this practice will enlighten you to the power of prayer. Or maybe this is not for you and that is okay. Peace to you. But like the spare tire, what if it could be?

### *I don't pray.*

Really? When your mother is dying in the hospital, you are pacing the halls, crying with doctors and you are desperate for healing power, who do you think is listening to your plea, hope, and *prayer*? When your thoughts go out to someone who struggles with loss or wrangling grief, your thoughts don't just evaporate. They are being channeled. They are divinely being applied. *They are prayers*. Here's the best reason you don't pray. You are angry or frustrated with a situation and yell, "Jesus H. Christ!" That's like flashing your high beams or honking your horn. Often we are making a divine connection and we don't even realize it.

### *I don't have faith.*

Surely you have faith or trust in something or someone. Maybe it's the silver beams of light emanating from a full moon, the intoxicating aromas of spring hyacinths, or the angelic smile on your baby's face. It's what you believe and what you feel.

Full disclosure: I am an open-minded, free-range, free-thinking, spiritual, self-proclaimed, convenience store Catholic. Maybe my belief system is not popular among the more devout, but I drive through and grab what I need. Maybe it is gas for my car. Or maybe it's just wiper fluid for a clean windshield. You can't drive without either. The point is I keep driving back because I am needy. Aren't we all? I also practice yoga, believe in the spirit world, love what mediums offer, and always look for signs from those in the afterlife. I have been told I am sensitive and intuitive. My faith is like a freshly lined road. Religion is on one side and spirituality is on the other. I've always been a center-of-the-road, yellow double-lines kind of gal. True story: when I was two years old, while playing outside in the fenced in backyard, I surprisingly discovered someone had left the gate unlocked. Curiosity got the best of me. Mind you, we lived in the country along a very busy road. No one was more surprised than my mom when the doorbell rang and a tractor trailer driver had me in his arms and told her he found me walking down the double yellow lines on the road. So I guess I learned the art of walking in the middle of the road at a very young age. A precursor perhaps to my belief system. Both sides are important to living, dying, losing, and grieving. My happy place is driving down the double yellow lines engaging with both sides of the road — pedal to the metal, top down, wind in my hair, and uninhibited reckless abandon. This is where self discovery happens, and trust begins. A reliance on faith is integral to living as it is to surviving loss.

And while I may debate some of the man made rules of religion — ask my mom, our conversations are often very spirited — I will always defend my faith. I have had people ask me why I remain a Catholic if I don't subscribe to all it preaches or expects — my convenience store comparison. My answer? I am perfectly imperfect. Religions are not one-size-fits-all. The only way I can try to affect change is to stay the course. Shift happens.

Tragedy can make the wheels fall off. I am forever grateful my mom and dad instilled a faithful foundation for us to build upon, rely on, and propel us forward. My dad was a mechanic to his core. He made us road-worthy, and mom kept fuel in our tanks. To this day mom makes sure she tops us off even when we think we don't need it. After a while it's up to each of us to decide which car to drive. And Fr. Frank kept us on the road with mindful prayer.

My faith in the Hail Mary and everything she stands for sustains me. It's like a kickstand or a mechanic's lift allowing closer inspection of the engine from all angles. It is my own personal, private, and holy reflection and a holy communication with the Divine. And like that kickstand? Faith is something to lean on, prop you up and keep you steady in good and bad times. Loss and grief are possibly the worst of times. Better to believe in something and be pleasantly surprised than believe in nothing to find out you wish you had. Here's the thing. Inflation may affect the cost of goods, services, and commodities, but it can never affect faith in mindful prayer. It is free and it is priceless, so invest.

And if you lead with your heart, respect others and judge less, the living like Mary and loving like Jesus effect wins every time. Isn't that the goal after all? Again, it doesn't matter the car you drive, it's the fuel in your tank. Are you filled up?

*Third Gear:*

# Driver's Ed

# 10

# What I Learned From My Dad, Grief, And Driving A Stick

Surviving Mary Ellen's death at first was like driving a car down the road with four wheels and no lug nuts. We were scared, wobbly, and worried about what would happen next. Our master mechanic's toolbox had been dumped all over the garage floor. Ever determined, "Lou the Glue" found the torque wrench and secured our wheels so we could feel steady, safe, and secure again. Dad worked tirelessly to inject joy back into our broken lives.

Growing up with a dad in the car business, our family did too. Mom worked there part-time, my brothers washed and detailed cars as kids, and I would go to work with my dad on Tuesday evenings after dinner. Sometimes I'd sit in Dad's office as he was closing a car deal with a customer. He could sell a car to anyone. Other times I would go to the parts department and take inventory with my eyes: engine parts, bolts, and belts. I'd wander into the mechanics' bays and watch them work magic with grease-stained hands. One of my favorite nostalgic smells is gasoline and fresh oil dripped on a garage floor. Most of the time, you could find me behind the wheel of a brand-new shiny car in the showroom. I'd press every button on the dashboard and pretend to be racing down a track. So, it's no surprise that we didn't huddle around the television set on Monday nights watching football, basketball, or the World Series.

My dad wasn't a jock. He was passionate about cars. We watched the Grand Prix, Formula One, the Indy and the Daytona 500 on television. Often this would parlay to the field next to our house and we would race around with field cars, motorcycles, or snowmobiles on the back nine of our property. I had two older brothers to chase and keep up with. Barbies were fine, but I always loved to send the "Sizzlers" down on my brothers' orange "Hot Wheels" racetrack in the basement when they weren't looking. Trying to tag along with them as they went off on their outside adventures was always my goal. I wasn't always successful. They had tree forts, and Dad built me a gingerbread house with a cedar roof and two ceramic elves outside of the cottage door. I felt like Snow White. The elf house was amazingly detailed and a little girl's dream. I loved it. But I always longed for a house in a tree.

Inherently being mechanical is a gift. It was in my dad's DNA. He was more like a surgeon, and the car was his patient. He was fastidious and always a perfectionist. It's true you must know your product inside and out before selling it. He passed that along to my brothers and me. And anything he owned with an engine, be it the Gravely tractor he used to plow the field for our outdoor playground to his white Ford Thunderbird that he adored right up until his final drive, he lovingly took care of.

Perhaps that gene is hereditary. While my brothers may have inherited Dad's mechanical astuteness, Dad taught me instincts of the car, knowing the sounds and feels of when things are good and not so good. My dad, being the eternal car enthusiast, thought every one of his kids should know how to drive a stick. I was no exception as it was a life skill his daughter should know. So, I learned at a young age. First, it was a Honda XR75 motorcycle, then an old Datsun.

Years later, my dad and I bought a 1967 convertible VW Bug. I always had an affinity with vintage VWs. Maybe it's being a child born in the 1960s. Maybe it's me trying to hold on to an era when my sister was still alive. Whatever the reason, when I found her, I knew it. She is the prettiest shade of yellow, like an underripe dandelion. We named her Sweet Pea. It was a vintage restoration project dad and I did together. Admittedly, Dad probably did more of the restoring and I did more of the driving. She still grinds while downshifting to second gear when going too fast. It's a reminder to be mindful when shifting. And while she yearns to keep up with traffic on the highway, going over fifty-five mph upsets her little engine. She has blown a piston or two over the years. Another mindful yet costly reminder that not knowing your own speed limit can have consequences.

As unforgettable as my dad will always be, the smile Sweet Pea put on his face whenever he was behind the wheel—top down and on the open road—was priceless. Joy is transcending and contagious because that is exactly my reaction, still. Now that Dad is gone, I am inherently reminded of his love for that car and him. The smell of the leather interior mixed with aromas of gasoline from the engine is forever vintage Volkswagen and immediately makes me think of my dad. Every time I start her up in the spring after her long winter's nap, I give my dad a wink and hope she starts.

My dad and Sweet Pea remind me that moving through grief is like learning to drive a stick shift with a vintage car. Knowing how to shift can come in handy, not simply driving your car but driving another's if they cannot or are struggling. You have to shift often and much while driving in life. You shift gears so the engine can slow down, speed up, and perform at its best.

Is it a "three on the tree" shifter mounted on the steering column or a "four on the floor"? Is the gear box a "dogleg" or "H" pattern? It can be confusing and overwhelming. There are many stops and stalls, like grief. Just when you get a feel for one, you find yourself behind the wheel of another you must navigate. Loss is inevitable, and we will have to endure many in our lifetime.

Dad always said shifting is a feeling and an understanding of the sounds of the engine. The more intimate you are with your car, the more you will trust your instinct when knowing to shift. But a stick requires mindful action. Automatic transmission does the work for you; convenient, yes, but grief never is. And if you don't shift gears, you will not get to where you need to go. A car in neutral goes nowhere. A person stuck in grief stays in limbo.

If you downshift at high speeds, you can damage the engine. Too fast or too slow affects performance. Gears will grind, which is uncomfortable as it loudly demonstrates to anyone you drive by that you haven't mastered shifting yet. It takes time, just like grief.

Reverse is for backing up or parking. You can't stay in reverse because you cannot relive or change the past. Dad always shifted through the gears and moved us forward. A smooth transition can be difficult to attain. Then you find yourself on a hill at a stoplight. You are sandwiched with cars in front and cars behind. Sweat starts to form on your brow. You've been here before. There is jerking forward and rolling backward. Your ability to balance one foot on the clutch and one on the gas pedal is pivotal. If you are not skilled enough, you will roll into the car behind you. If you give it too much gas when releasing the clutch, you will ram the car in front of you. The engine is revving, and with a slight lift of the left foot and a gentle push of the right foot, your car is holding and hovering the uphill hold, the sweet spot, as you remain buried between the other cars. The light turns green; you take a deep breath, slowly release the clutch, and push the accelerator. It's clumsy but you climb the hill, turn on your blinker, and take the turn. Eventually your feet find their rhythm and they learn to dance until it's a part of you.

That's what grief is in life. You will start, stop, and stall out. You will hold on a hill and then roll backward. There is no shortcut or toll road on this grief journey. The road is long, filled with potholes, detours, and construction. Engage with that spiritual compass to find your faithful bearings; let it direct you to your True North and onward to the open road because it waits for you, but you must mindfully shift.

# 11 Check-Engine Light Is On

Misfortune and death seem to affect every family at one time or another. Loss is a common denominator among us. And if we have faith, we know we will see our loved ones again, but when we begin our grief journey, it feels like that reunion will take forever. That is why I am overly redundant with the reaching out and reaching in concept. It is pivotal, if not crucial, to healing. Let's be honest; death makes us clumsy. We don't want to intrude, but we don't want to exclude, right?

When your check engine light comes on, your reaction is usually S#!t! It's never a good sign, usually. You can't ignore it, for it could signal serious engine failure to the annoying O2 sensor. So you must address it. Like others' losses, at times, we feel awkward and hardly know what to say, what to do, or how to act.

One thing is certain, you will always be remembered for your kindness, your presence, a kind word, a gentle smile, a shared memory, or an embrace. So, if you are struggling with what to do when someone needs support during tough times—lend a hand, provide a shoulder, make that casserole, attend that funeral, give a call, or send a sympathy card. And if you run into someone at the grocery store who recently lost a loved one, don't dodge them; indulge them. Don't let your feeling uncomfortable make them feel worse. Trust me; they already feel uncomfortable with their loss. When my dad was dying, my cousin shared with me the concept of "holding space." This is when you are present physically, mentally, and emotionally. It's giving all you've got in that moment for another, with no judgement. It's the epitome of empathy. And that is a gift. There is a reason the side mirrors on a car have "Objects in the mirror are closer than they appear." Loss is bigger to us than anyone else. Your actions, words, and kind deeds will be remembered forever. It's what you don't do that will never be forgotten.

Somehow, though, written words, to me, can have lasting impact. I am a bit of a sentimental pack rat. I save greeting cards—the special ones. I have a box filled with sentiments from my husband over our 30 plus year relationship, my dad's loving words in perfect penmanship from birthdays, college letters of support, or that amazingly tearful toast he gave at my wedding. Tucked in that box are also cards from my mom, homemade ones from my kids, and some from family and friends too special to recycle. I cherish some I received after my dad passed away. The words are indelible like fresh dripped oil left behind long after a car leaves a driveway. The puddle fades over time but the outline or shadow remains. It is always comforting to read and reread the lives touched by someone, and in my sister's case, someone gone too soon.

The following thoughtful words were extended to my parents way-back-when:

> **"...I am praying to Mary Ellen for help, to raise our sons to be as close to God as she. Such a blessing for her family to know they've an angel in heaven. We are expecting our 4th in March and are hoping for a girl. If it be God's will we get her — I pray she'll be every bit like Mary Ellen." CHC**

> **"...We care and share your sorrow, although we have never met. We have two little saints now — John was three and Annie was five — and at the time we were going through the adjustment and acceptance of their not being there to hold, it seemed to give all the pain and sorrow some meaning to know that others shared the feeling and perhaps looked at their own children in a new light of appreciation." MH**

> **"...God has sent you four perfect rosebuds to nurture and cultivate. You have given Him back one in full bloom and unblemished — a perfect rose." PK**

The nun that cared for my brothers and me during those three days captures our transition aptly:

> **"...The events of this one week still stagger me—the little girl we never met that brought together people who would have never dreamed of coming together in so close and united a relationship; people who have been so deeply concerned and anxious to help in some way, who**

have offered their prayers, and even their tears, to you who belonged to her and loved her to the giving of your own death (for truly you did die many a death in your futile efforts to save her and in those long, patient, loving hours you spent watching by her bed).

People I met the last few days in the store, the post office, and the filling station asked about Mary Ellen. They did not say much but expressed very much by a shake of the head or an "ah." The clerk in the drug store was telling another Sister how impressed one of the doctors had been. He is not a Catholic. In her own unique way, Mary Ellen was an effective missionary.

In the days to come, you will feel loneliness and pain. That is to be. Do not try to hide these feelings from those whom you love—your children, your family, your friends—because all know this must be part of you and they can help you only if you show them the aching in your hearts. Your children will be able to understand and help heal the hurt only if you let them feel the intensity in your hearts that tells them they too are loved and needed by you.

Mary Ellen is very near all of you, I am sure, and many times now, I feel her presence. She is not gone from you, just present in a different manner.

**I cannot tell you how much I admired your beautiful expression of faith during this sorrow." MS**

# 12 Reflections From The Rearview Mirror

Moving on from that Denver morning was challenging for our family, relatives, and friends. We all use a rearview mirror while driving to see what's behind us and for backing up in reverse so that we can navigate space while parking. While we can't rewind our past, we can find ways to shift through it and find meaning. Here are some shared reflections that are a testament that life, love, and the eternal transcend.

### *From Alice Le Brun, Mary Ellen's Mother*

At my age, fifty years ago can seem like yesterday. To know that I am eighty-nine years old and that my daughter, Mary Ellen, would be sixty-six this year shows how time is fleeting. Often that is how I feel when I reflect upon the day my beautiful daughter died. My heart forever aches but is softened by the years in between. To lose a child is devastating. The loss you are feeling is indescribable. Your whole life is changed forever. Your sorrow is so deep, and your life is shattered.

How can you go on? How can you survive this tragedy? You wonder why this has happened. You ask God, why? But there is no answer. They say our children are only loaned to us. Only God knows the answer.

When my brother, Fr. Frank Taney, wrote the original booklet and dedicated it to Mary Ellen, he compared our family's life to a beautiful tapestry, highlighting that if we didn't have the dark shades in it, the tapestry would not be as beautiful. This is true, I know now, but at the time, it was difficult to understand. My faith in God has always been strong, but I found that I had to work so hard to accept this loss, as any mother would. Each day was like climbing a mountain, sometimes it would be good, and other days you would slide right back down to the bottom. Faith is a gift, but when we are tested, we have to work so hard to keep it. I believe God has a plan for each of us. Sometimes it isn't always what we want. But we have to accept it. And although acceptance can take a lifetime, once we do, our Lord will help us carry our cross.

My personal journey to accept my daughter's death was difficult. I read many books about people who had lost a child to see how they got through it. One day, I remember crying at the weight of her loss and saying to God that I would accept this cross if you would help me to carry it. At that moment, peace and tranquility came over me. I trusted that God would help me and be there for me. The old adage "sink or swim" came to mind; my wonderful husband Lou and my three beautiful children, David, Stephen, and Michelle, needed me to be present in their lives. I will always be forever grateful for my husband, Lou, who kept our family moving forward. And to my family and friends: each phone call, letter, or personal visit provided mortar to sustain. Life had to move forward, and I welcomed each distraction until it wasn't.

My brother, Fr. Frank, assured me that I would find meaning and purpose in my grief by reaching out to others who have lost a child. Each time I did, though, my own sorrow would resurface. However, sharing my pain fortified my heart in the process. The cross became easier to carry. Helping others helped me. Without my faith, I would have nothing to hold onto. It will forever be paramount to accept my sorrows.

I have always prayed the traditional Rosary. But praying Mary Ellen's Rosary makes me feel connected to Mary Ellen as she loved it, but it also puts me in the presence of the Virgin Mary because the virtues meditated on are examples of her virtuous life. Mary Ellen's Rosary was a part of our family's life. Her original booklet has helped so many people. It is a beautiful way to pray the Rosary. While praising Our Lady through prayer, you are asking her to intercede and implement her virtues in your life. Praying the Hail Mary full of life in this way also provides me with a personal connection to Mary Ellen because I know how much it meant to her in her final days.

I am perpetually inspired by Mary, our Blessed Mother who committed no sin, and yet her cross to bear was the crucifixion of her Son, Jesus. She accepted her suffering, as did Jesus upon his death, a death to save all of us. If you believe in his death, then through it comes deep faith. I am comforted and look forward to being reunited with Mary Ellen and all of my loved ones again. Our time here is brief, and we must offer up our crosses and sufferings to God along the way.

Our faith is a beautiful gift. Acceptance, love, and forgiveness are so much a part of our faith. Cherish your faith and never take it for granted. If you continue to water it, it will grow and be there for you when you thirst for spiritual guidance. God and our Blessed Mother and our faith will sustain us. I truly believe this as it has guided my path throughout my life. I am touched that this book is renewed and will continue to be a lifeline for others.

### *From Dave Le Brun, Mary Ellen's Brother*

Prayer was a common thread in our family, and it was woven throughout our lives. Our faith was challenged that summer of 1969 on our family vacation of a lifetime. The Badlands, Mount Rushmore, and the Grand Canyon would be fleeting as our journey would soon take a detour.

When my sister's tragedy unfolded, we had no idea how much we would need prayer and depend on God in those early morning hours that Sunday or the next three days and for the rest of our lives. And no matter how hard you pray, God doesn't always give you the answer you desire.

My sister Mary Ellen was the kindest, softest sister you could have; we rarely fought. She was just so nice to be around. She and Mom were so close. After losing her, life was such a blur. I just remember we lost our sister, didn't know why or how this could have happened, and wondered what was going to happen next.

I have learned that when a tragedy like this happens, we all grieve on our own level and that God will not give us more than we can handle. This definitely occurred with me. But it became so quiet and lonely around our house. Sure, people came over all the time, but that didn't fill the void we were feeling. It was a good thing Fr. Frank was transferred to Buffalo only a few hours away. He was a regular presence in our home and as kids we loved it. He was larger than life itself. He helped us heal.

Around the same time, my good friend's family suffered a loss, and the sadness was too much to bear, and his parents divorced. I wondered if this was going to happen in my family because of losing Mary Ellen. It made me feel unsure and afraid. I would sometimes find my mom in her bedroom, in the middle of the day, just sobbing. It was a really painful time for our family. My mom insisted we pray the Rosary together on Sunday nights, and Dad's strength and faith were so strong. He was "the glue" that kept our family together.

But here's the takeaway. I mentioned earlier that prayer was always in our life. And we all participated. I witnessed God bringing my parents even closer together than they already were, and the bond was evidently so strong. I felt safe and confident knowing that our family was going to endure this tragedy—and with Mary Ellen being the strength between us all. My dad became the pillar of strength for the family—I felt there was no force that he couldn't protect us from. I was sure Mary Ellen had some part of this. My parents making prayer a part of our daily lives gave us all the tools we needed to deal with the loss of Mary Ellen. Yes, we all did it differently, but I do not know how we would have survived without it. And I continue to say Mary Ellen's Rosary to this day.

Moving forward many years, I wonder what seeing Mary Ellen will be like when my time to leave this earth occurs. But I bet she's as beautiful as I remember her to be. She will be there with my dad, Lou, and my younger son, Andrew, and my favorite uncle, Fr. Frank. I remember my dad's strength during those early days and throughout tough times in our lives. I knew then that was the man I wanted to be. I just didn't know that I, too, would walk the same path as him.

I lost my son Andrew in 2018 and wonder when I will ever feel steady again. But I draw upon my dad's example each and every day. Like my parents, each time my wife and I reach out to provide comfort to others in their losses, we find a little more peace in ours. It will take a lifetime; of that, I'm sure. I rely on my faith. I count on Mary Ellen's Rosary that gave my sister peace to give me the same in time.

I am forever thankful and blessed with my wonderful wife, Terry, and my thoughtful son, Philip, who is always there. We know how powerful prayer can be. I will end by saying that God has His plan, and we all have a beginning and end time, all determined by Him. Things happen for reasons that we may not understand now. We will get those answers someday as to why we lost loved ones, sometimes so early in life. There are no coincidences, and God holds the master key.

### *From Steve Le Brun, Mary Ellen's Brother*

> *Hail Mary full of life, the lord is with you.* Guiding *are you among women and* guiding *is the fruit of your womb, Jesus. Holy Mary, Mother of God, pray for us to be* guiding *now and at the hour of our death, Amen.*

As an adult, I no longer blame God for my sister's death. God doesn't take loved ones from us. Life does. Life is what happens the moment we come to being. Life gives life, and life takes life. Life is the reason people die, get into accidents, fall deathly ill, or die horribly wrong. That is life.

But as a nine-year-old boy who lost his sister in 1969 because my family was getting ready to go to church, I blamed God. I really hated what happened to our family. The only reason we were in that hotel was so we could freshen up from the week of camping and go to church that morning. I associated getting ready and going to church with Mary Ellen's death. I had so many questions and no answers.

What is even more strange is I remember a few months prior on Easter on our way home from Mass once again we were all in the ole Chrysler, and my dad rounded an S turn at around 30 mph, and Mary Ellen was sitting by the door, and the door flew open, and she almost was thrown from the car. She could have gotten badly injured, run over by a car, or even killed. Was God saving her for a higher purpose? Looking back, it would seem so.

I have asked myself over the years, why does something like this happen, especially when one is readying themselves to go worship the Lord in church?

We were a religious family before Mary Ellen died. We remained so after her death. While we were connected in our faith and praying Mary Ellen's Rosary and going to church on Sundays, I felt disconnected. I was an altar boy, went to church, and attended Catholic school, yet I struggled serving God. Maybe it was part of the grieving process. We never talked about Mary Ellen's death until years later. Maybe it was the fear of opening deeply buried wounds? Dave, Michelle, and I wanted normalcy that we would never achieve, no matter how hard we tried. It was our new normal. There was no manual for us as a family to navigate through this terrible grief. There were no podcasts or people focus groups.

I love my parents. The love and support they gave us our entire lives was constant. Each of us had our way of dealing with the grief, and it can take a lifetime. And it took most of ours to talk about her death. My sister was such a beautiful soul. To have her as our connection in this way is a gift.

My parents' faith in God was strong and awesome. I believe in God, I am spiritual, and I pray. I have great faith, and I can thank my parents for that, but I don't believe I need to sit in a pew to communicate with God. My mom has struggled with this belief, but she was and continues to be a great example of a faithful person. Our religious rituals may not be the same, but our path is. Experiencing personal tragedy can have you questioning a lot of things. But if your faith is deep, God will find a way to help you heal. And your journey is personal.

Sometimes I reflect back and think of the symbolism that I perceived to have occurred back on that terrible day. I remember the group of kids saying, "Watch out; something bad is gonna happen" at a stoplight in downtown Denver. The hotel we stayed at was right next door to the hospital. The number three resonates with me. There were two other people along with Jesus who were placed on crosses for a total of three. Jesus was crucified on the cross and rose again after three days. The Holy Trinity (three): the Father, Son, and Holy Spirit. As my sister's accident was happening, I ran through the hallway and knocked on three hotel room doors to get help, and it was the third door that opened. It took three men to remove the three hinge pins from the three hinges on that bathroom door. Mary Ellen just turned thirteen; she died three days later of third-degree burns on 90 percent of her body on July 30. Where there were four children in our family had now become three. Is there any symbolism here? Or am I just trying to make sense out of something completely senseless?

I am in my sixties, and still, I miss my sister. I am thankful for having my own family, for my three children, Ronna, Reid, and Chase, and for my life partner, Petra. I believe Mary Ellen's death and the Rosary she loved hearing Fr. Frank say with her at her dying bedside had some purpose. Something positive must come from that. I believe her suffering and her story have helped other families and people cope with the loss of loved ones. I believe there is something in all of this that has happened to our family that can help others heal their souls, comfort their losses, or reconnect with their spiritual God. I hope that in the afterlife, I can join and celebrate life everlasting with my sister, my father, my grandparents, my nephew, my aunts and uncles and cousins who have gone before us, and I hope I can have the people in my earthly life now alongside with me then.

I hope that this continuation of the story of Mary Ellen and the Rosary she loved helps people of all walks of life. This virtuous version allows a person to actually engage their current thought or feeling into the Hail Mary prayer by allowing them to add different virtues needed instead of repeating the same chant over and over. If you are seeking patience or understanding, or forgiveness, or if you need guidance or if you are feeling thankful—any word you can think of you add to the prayer. It makes it a more personal prayer experience.

Finally, regardless of your affiliation of faith, in the grand theme of eternal life, there is only One God Almighty, and we should never get caught up in the religious differences we may have, as those differences can only distract and take us away from Him. In Jesus's name, Amen.

> *Hail Mary full of life, the Lord is with you. Accepting are you among women and accepting is the fruit of your womb, Jesus. Holy Mary, Mother of God, pray for us to be accepting now and at the hour of our death. Amen.*

### *From Bernadette Taney Irving, Mary Ellen's Cousin*

At two years my senior, my cousin Mary Ellen was like a sister to me. Our families were close, spending lots of time together, birthdays, holidays, sleepovers, going on adventures together, even taking our first plane ride together. I looked up to her; she was smart, thoughtful, lots of fun, and very tolerant of her younger cousin.

In hindsight, I can see how mature she was for her age. I have a very clear memory of one Sunday when I attended mass with Mary Ellen. As I fidgeted and struggled to sit still and wondered when it would be over, I remember looking at her, sitting quietly, focused, and attentive to the mass. At that moment, I remember wanting to be just like her.

I was eleven years old when we received the call that my dear cousin had been severely injured. It was devastating. I can remember standing in my backyard, looking up to the stars and pleading with God to heal her. Under the same sky, three nights later, I was asking God why He couldn't spare her.

My life was changed forever, and I believe I am still trying to heal from the pain of her loss. However, her life, though short, touched so many. Her unbelievable strength and unwavering faith in God while enduring so much pain and suffering remains an inspiration for us all.

It was especially comforting for me when my uncle, a Maryknoll missionary who spent those last days with Mary Ellen, shared with me the New Rosary for Young People, explaining how it had given her so much comfort in her time of need. I quickly learned it and have never said the Rosary any other way since. It brings personal meaning to each Hail Mary by focusing on a particular virtue that has meaning for me in my life, but also because it connects me with the spirit of my beautiful cousin.

### *From Doris Taney, Mary Ellen's Aunt*

Whenever I say the Rosary, I think of Mary Ellen. She was my niece and my daughter's best friend as well as her cousin. She was sweet, thoughtful, kind, and fun to have around.

Her love for praying the Rosary with the virtues making it personal is understandable and relatable. It is so easy to make each bead belong to the person or situation you are praying for.

I am thankful to Fr. Frank and Mary Ellen for bringing it to reality.

### *From Teresa Coggins Nicosia, Mary Ellen's Best Friend*

I recently reread the original book, *Mary Ellen's New Rosary for Young People*. I was definitely brought back to that summer of 1969. I, like Mary Ellen, was thirteen. So many emotions—disbelief, shock, helplessness, overwhelming sadness, fear, feeling numb. And the memories—the phone call from Fr. O'Connell asking us to pray for Mary Ellen, my mother telling me what had happened, not being able to cry, going to the funeral home with my parents before the calling hours, seeing Mr. and Mrs. Le Brun standing by the casket, seeing Mary Ellen in a dress and white gloves. As I write, the images become more clear, painfully clear. It's interesting how the years can soften and bury those difficult memories.

However, as I remember my childhood friend, it's brought me much comfort and reassurance that Mary Ellen has remained a huge presence in my life. I have certainly prayed to her over the years. Mary Ellen has helped me get through so much, from what seemed to be monumental as a teenager and young adult to dealing with and accepting some painful and difficult challenges in my adult life.

Mary Ellen was the nicest person around. She and I were classmates at St. Mary's School from the first through sixth grades. We both loved ice cream sandwiches for lunch in the cafeteria. We played together on the playground, and sometimes we ran to my house next to the school to see my babysitter, Mrs. Hart. We loved being in our third-grade play, *Mary Poppins*, singing "A Spoonful of Sugar" over and over. We wore sparkly angel wings and halos made from gold tinsel for the Christmas pageants. We made our First Communion together. We got nervous together, waiting for Fr. O'Connell to call our names and give us our report cards in class, waiting with hands folded on our desks. Mary Ellen always did very well. I did okay but sometimes talked too much.

We both enjoyed being together in school, but we also spent lots of time at each other's houses. I was the youngest of four in my family. Mary Ellen was the oldest of four. (At that time, I was envious of her being the oldest of her siblings. Now, I'm quite happy to be the youngest of mine!) I loved being at her house—playing duets on the piano, working on school projects, and especially playing with her baby sister, Michelle. When I stayed overnight, Mr. Le Brun would sometimes bring Michelle into Mary Ellen's bedroom early in the morning before Mary Ellen woke up, so I could play with Michelle. I remember seeing *The Sound of Music* in 1965 with Mary Ellen, twice! It was such a big excursion. We went to the theater in Syracuse with her parents, then again with mine. We were mesmerized by Maria, and we loved the intermission when the big red curtain closed. I'm sure we wore our favorite dresses! To this day, when I watch *The Sound of Music*, I think of Mary Ellen and the impact that movie had on us.

I'm holding a small round cedar box in my hand to give me inspiration as I reflect on Mary Ellen. Mr. and Mrs. Le Brun gave it to me that summer after Mary Ellen died. She bought it as a souvenir when they were on their trip. She wrote on the bottom of it in pencil, in perfect St. Mary's handwriting, "Mt.

Rushmore, July, Black Hills, South Dakota." I have always kept my childhood charm bracelet in that little box, and I cherish both. I always will.

I feel so fortunate that the Le Brun family has always remained a special and influential part of my life. They have celebrated milestones with me: graduations, my wedding, births of my children. I'll always remember Mr. Le Brun meeting a guy I was dating while going to Nazareth College. When he took us out to dinner, Mr. Le Brun made it very clear that he didn't really think that guy was right for me. A few years later, he met another guy, Peter, who was a car guy. Of course, he approved of him, and I married that one.

My mother and father always said the Rosary. It was an important part of our family life from as far back as I can remember. My mother's devotion to the Blessed Mother was instilled in us at an early age. We said Grace then the Hail Mary every night before dinner. We said the Rosary as a family on every car trip. I learned to say Novenas for special intentions from my mother. Needless to say, I was very familiar with the Rosary before *Mary Ellen's New Rosary for Young People* was published over fifty years ago. However, the substitution of different virtues for "blessed" was especially meaningful for me at the age of thirteen.

I also felt a special connection to Mary Ellen by saying "her" Rosary, knowing how much she prayed the Rosary those three July days. I'm sure the virtues I used then were to help me accept and understand my friend's death. I may have substituted words such as comforting, caring, guiding, or faithful for "blessed." Over the years, I have continued to say the Rosary for certain intentions, but with few changes to the Hail Mary.

Now that I have revisited the list of virtues for Mary Ellen's Rosary, I realize there are many virtues that would be especially meaningful during this challenging time of struggle and uncertainty in the world.

I think about Mary Ellen often, especially on her birthday, July 16. She would be sixty-six now. I imagine us getting together, drinking wine, talking about Medicare options, sharing pictures of our families, and trying to keep up with the endless technology changes as true boomers. I know we would be bringing our mothers out to lunch, reminiscing with them about their lives, our lives. Although I can't have lunch with my dear childhood friend, these written reflections have made me realize Mary Ellen is with me in spirit. She always has been. She always will be.

### *From The McQuillan Family*

Dear Le Brun Family,

Mary Ellen has walked by our sides for most of our lives. She has comforted us through many difficult times and celebrated many more triumphs and joyous days. She has come to us in our dreams; we were told stories and have memories of calming messages filled with faith, humility, anticipation, and, of course, prayer.

Faith: Complete trust and belief. A frame hung in our childhood home that held the palms every Lent for decades also held Mary Ellen's photo. This made her legendary to us, and her presence is held dearly in our hearts and minds.

Humility: Love seems like an easy thing to do and feel. To be able to love unconditionally for your family and friends can be.

Mary Ellen and Fr. Frank showed us how to love all through their actions. They looked upon the not-so-loved, perhaps—the unfortunate, sick, and poor decision-makers. They threw love out to everyone, laughter being a comforting conduit.

Anticipation: The messages sent from Heaven that this is not our final home, but we have so much in which to look forward! They set examples for us to work on in hopes we can meet them again.

Prayer: *Mary Ellen's New Rosary* book changed the way we pray and, for some of us, made it more acceptable to pray out loud. Her book also made it more interesting, with the suggestion of substituting words and customizing your prayer. After Mary Ellen's death, our family added her Hail Mary after our evening grace. Many of us still do and hope that it will also carry to our next generation.

How to summarize the impact Mary Ellen and Fr. Frank have had on our lives is a bit difficult to put that feeling in words. Simply know, so many lives have been and continue to be graced by their time on earth.

### *From Teresa Donovan Cotter, Mary Ellen's Cousin*

It all started with Father Frank. In 1966, when my then eleven-year-old brother Joe came home from a scouting trip late on a Sunday afternoon, Dad took him to an evening Mass across the river at Holy Rosary in Portland, Oregon. A Maryknoll priest, Frank Taney, who was originally from New York and a visitor to the church, preached at the Mass. Dad wondered if he might be a relative. After all, Dad's grandmother was Catherine Taney. A joyful conversation after Mass revealed that Father Frank's grandfather was

Felix Taney, Catherine's brother! Dad explained it as "Divine Providence." Father Frank came to our house the next day to see the old family photos. What a gift! Cousins in New York we did not even know we had, including Father Frank, and lots of others we had yet to meet, including Mary Ellen and her little sister, Michelle.

Mary Ellen and I are days apart in age. Though I knew her briefly, she changed my life. Shortly after her tragic death, I was confirmed. My confirmation name is Mary Ellen. I have always felt her near. Her prayers have always been a help.

This beautiful sequel has Michelle Le Brun sharing her compelling Mary Ellen story. I see the two sisters as bookends. The story of Mary Ellen was waiting to be told by the one who was meant to tell it, Michelle. All in God's time. I hear my dad saying, "Divine Providence." I believe her story and the Rosary can bring you close to the hearts of Jesus and Mary and bring you to a peace that no one else can give. Mary Ellen, pray for us.

### *From The Author To Her Sister*

People say you can't miss what you never had. I had you for four years. So *that* could not be further from the truth. They say a little child could hardly remember something so tragic. Take a walk in my memories. It's all there. One minute I was being held in your arms, entangled in sheets, sharing a hotel bed, the next, you were gone forever. The permanence of this shift was just beginning for me. The moments between replayed the nightmare in my mind. There was a wake and a funeral. I didn't get to attend. Too young, they thought. But I needed closure because I couldn't figure out where you went and when you were coming back. I had to grow into that reality. It took most of a lifetime.

Dad could fix everything and anything, but he couldn't fix this. He did repair our lives, though. He kept the gas tank full so we could always move forward, and when we broke down, he always had the tools to get us back on the road to living. Several years after you died, Dad put in an in ground swimming pool and an addition to our home with a master suite and formal dining room. The pool gave us endless summertime happiness and the addition gave everyone their own bedroom. Dave got Mom and Dad's, Steve got mine, and I shifted to yours. It made sense because yours was already preordained with white furniture and fluffy yellow chenille bedding, as it was your favorite color.

Dad created a dining room with beautiful details—handmade wide plank floors, velveteen wallpaper, white wainscoting, a dining room table that could accommodate the last supper, and a life-like painted portrait of you and your gentle smile. It was an homage. There was a brass light over your image, and you would glow during dinner and often long after we cleared the table. Having you on the wall made you a part of the celebrations and holidays that eventually grew to be happy.

I wanted my own picture of you for my new bedroom, so I went down to the basement and searched endlessly in boxes and trunks until I found a little one. You were probably in fifth grade. Your hair was straight, and your cat-eye glasses were light blue with sparkles. The picture of you was the size of a half-dollar coin in a circular gilded frame. It forever sat upon my desk in my bedroom growing up, which used to be yours. That little photo has traveled with me to college and

Washington, DC. It now rests on the mantle above the fireplace. You are smiling next to Fr. Frank.

I also have a picture of us.

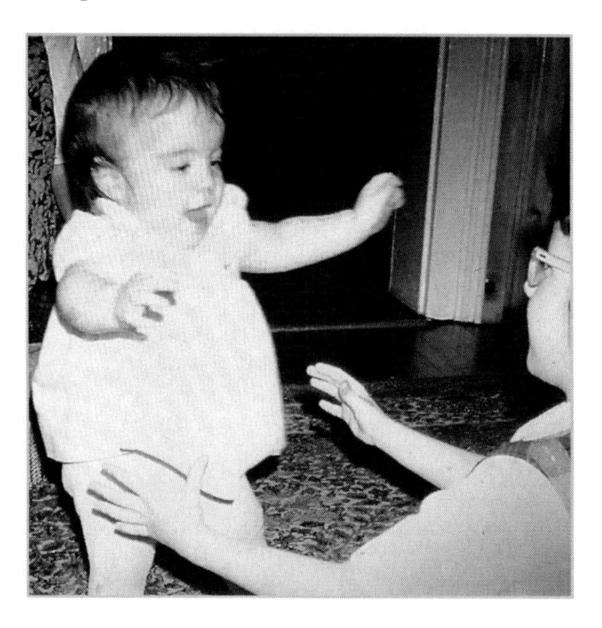

I am taking some first baby steps toward you. A smile on my face and your arms open wide. Sometimes it still feels that way, you and me. Although I imagine me falling into your arms and we are laughing. You are my big sister. But because of a fateful shift, we missed out on so much. We couldn't share stories. I couldn't come to you for advice on my period, boy crushes, or mean girls. You could not be in my wedding or share my joy being pregnant with the twins.

I missed the sisterhood shared stories of raising babies to toddlers to teenagers to young adults to college students. I know that is why I have "sister friends." They haven't taken your place but I am blessed you put them in my path. Losing Dad was so painful, we could not cry together uncontrollably in each other's arms. You are not here to go to lunch with Mom and me as we all grow older. Shift happens and life moves on. Mine certainly has in big and small ways.

I have felt your presence throughout my life, though, as if we are parallel parked in time, another time. I have always felt your hands on my shoulders, guiding me in the right direction, my proverbial blinker of sorts. You most likely have prevented me from taking a left turn or two in my life. The big sister-little sister connection transcends after all. I have talked to you when I am alone, prayed to you in silence, cried for you in my sleep, and reached for you in my dreams.

Back in 2007, when Dad's heart surgery caused uncontrollable bleeding, I walked down a long dark hallway in the hospital and made a deal with you that night. I knew I had Dad for all my forty-five years at that time, and you had only had him for thirteen. But selfishly I needed him more. My five-year-old twins, Margaux and Michael, needed their "Papa Louie" and I needed my dad. I could feel you pulling for him. He thankfully recovered, but I knew he was on borrowed time. It was eleven years later when Dad took his last breath. I said to him as he hovered between you and us that Holy Thursday evening that you were waiting for him, and it was your turn now. It felt so bittersweet. I was almost envious of your imminent reunion. Going on without him seemed a monumental shift, and it still is.

But I knew that telling him to grab your hand would give him the permission to cross over. He would finally be with the daughter he could not save on that fateful day. It turns out, no one could. After you died, you appeared to him in a dream, telling him you were okay, giving him peace. He couldn't be your hero that day, but he would forever be ours for the rest of his life. Oddly, losing you but saving us might have been his life's biggest reward as a father.

Undoubtedly, Fr. Frank had the perfect role model of inspiration to recycle a traditional prayer. Your *gentle, kind, loving, thoughtful,* and *peaceful* soul motivated him to breathe life into something old and create something new. Your approach to life was his blueprint. Its lasting effect on the lives of others is epic. Fearless leaders of change are remembered in history books. You, Mary Ellen, will be forever remembered in our family's "holy grail," our history book, our treasure chest. This is your legacy, your lingering and lasting effect.

Mary Ellen, I miss you, but I know deep down in my soul you have always been with me. You have always been my moral barometer. Righting the wrongs is a baton you shifted to me. And with that was and is a big responsibility to honor you in everything I did and do to this day. I may not always get it right, but I sure feel inspired by you when I come close.

To think of all the lives left untouched if things turned out differently is profound. Fr. Frank would not have found divine inspiration to create a youthful and more living version of the Rosary that was dedicated to you. The original "little red booklet" with your face adorning the cover would never have existed. It would not have been shared throughout the world. It would not be rolled up and rubber-banded and tattered by Mom's bed table, serving as her devotional prayer ritual each night since you died. Mom and Dad would not have reached out to others who lost a child, providing relief to others' grief. I would not be inspired to write this sequel *Holy Shift!* nor have your legacy to continue to share with others. So perhaps it's true, all things happen as they should. If our family's journey of losing you, being broken down, getting back on the road helps just one soul through loss, then all the cathartic pain in composing this book was worth it. Of that, I am certain. It's no coincidence that my VW Bug is yellow, is it?

*Fourth Gear:*

# The Road Map to Praying Mary Ellen's Rosary

While I believe the Hail Mary full of life can spiritually affect your attitude, latitude, and magnitude you may want more. If you are new to the Rosary, here is a road map to praying it. This version is an open invitation for anyone who needs a lifetime or a moment of peace. Godspeed on your journey through whatever loss you are wrangling. Peace and healing to you.

## The Mysteries

The mysteries provide the foundation for the Rosary. They represent the seasons of Jesus's life. The Joyful, the Sorrowful, the Glorious, and the Luminous share the stories of Jesus's trials, sufferings, and struggles. They also share his promise of love and everlasting life and the reverence of his mother, the Blessed Virgin Mary. The mysteries can be applied to different days of the week when you pray the Rosary. For example: the Joyful Mysteries may be prayed on Monday and Saturday, the Sorrowful on Tuesday and Friday, the Glorious on Wednesday and Sunday, and the Luminous on Thursday. When we pray the Rosary, we also meditate on the trials and tribulations of Jesus's life and perhaps how ours connect with his.

*The Joyful Mysteries*

1. The Annunciation: The angel Gabriel shares with Mary that she has been chosen to be the mother of Jesus.
2. The Visitation: Mary visits her cousin, Elizabeth.
3. The Nativity: Jesus is born in a stable in Bethlehem.
4. The Presentation: Mary and Joseph present the infant Jesus to God in the Temple.
5. The Finding of Jesus in the Temple: Mary and Joseph find Jesus in the Temple discussing his faith.

*The Sorrowful Mysteries*

1. The Agony in the Garden: Jesus prays in the Garden of Gethsemane.
2. The Scourging at the Pillar: Jesus is brutally lashed with whips.
3. The Crowning with Thorns: Jesus is mocked and receives a crown of thorns.
4. The Carrying of the Cross: Jesus carries the cross used to crucify him.
5. The Crucifixion: Jesus is nailed to the cross and dies.

*The Glorious Mysteries*

1. The Resurrection: Jesus is raised from the dead.
2. The Ascension: Jesus ascends to return to his Father in heaven.
3. The Coming of the Holy Spirit: The Holy Spirit descends to bring new life and power to the disciples.
4. The Assumption of Mary: Mary is taken, body and soul, to heaven.
5. The Coronation of Mary: Mary is crowned Queen of Heaven and Earth.

*The Luminous Mysteries*

1. The Baptism of Jesus: God declares Jesus his beloved Son.
2. The Wedding Feast at Cana: At Mary's urging, Jesus performs his first miracle.
3. The Proclamation of the Kingdom of God: Jesus brings the good news about the Kingdom of God.
4. The Transfiguration of Jesus: Jesus is revealed to Peter, James, and John in supernatural glory.
5. The Institution of the Eucharist: Jesus presents his Body and Blood to the disciples at the Last Supper.

**Praying the Rosary:**

Bless yourself with the sign of the cross:

*In the name of the Father, the Son, and the Holy Spirit. Amen.*

Start with "The Apostles Creed" prayer:

*I believe in God, the Father Almighty, Creator of heaven and earth, and in Jesus Christ, His only Son, our Lord. Who was conceived by the Holy Spirit, born of the Virgin Mary, suffered under Pontius Pilate, was crucified, died, and was buried. He descended into hell; the third day, He arose again from the dead; He ascended into heaven, sits at the right hand of God, the Father Almighty; from thence He shall come to judge the living and the dead. I believe in the Holy Spirit, the holy Catholic Church, the communion of saints, the forgiveness of sins, the resurrection of the body, and life everlasting. Amen.*

On the first large bead, say the "Our Father" prayer:

*Our Father, Who art in heaven, hallowed be Thy name. Thy kingdom come; Thy will be done on earth, as it is in heaven. Give us this day our daily bread; and forgive us our trespasses, as we forgive those who trespass against us. And lead us not into temptation but deliver us from evil. Amen.*

On the three small beads, say three mindful "Hail Marys" to increase faith, hope, and love.

> *Hail Mary, full of life; the Lord is with you, loving (or insert whatever virtue you need) are you among women, and loving is the fruit of your womb, Jesus. Holy Mary, Mother of God, pray for us to be loving now and at the hour of our death. Amen.*

Then recite the "Glory Be to the Father" prayer:

> *Glory be to the Father, and to the Son, and to the Holy Spirit; as it was in the beginning, is now, and ever shall be, world without end. Amen.*

Start the first decade of ten beads by meditating on the First Mystery.

- On the large bead, say the "Our Father."
- On the ten small beads, say ten mindful "Hail Marys."
- Then recite one "Glory Be to the Father."
- Then recite the "O My Jesus" prayer:
  *O my Jesus, forgive us our sins. Save us from the fires of hell. Lead all souls into heaven, especially those in most need of thy mercy. Amen.*

Say the rest of the Five Decades, each time meditating on one of the Mysteries.

At the end of the Five Decades, recite the "Hail Holy Queen" prayer:

> *Hail, Holy Queen, Mother of mercy, our life, our sweetness, and our hope! To thee do we cry, poor banished children of Eve; to thee do we send up our sighs, mourning, and weeping in this valley of tears. Turn then, most gracious advocate, thine eyes of mercy toward us: and after this our exile, show unto us the blessed fruit of thy womb, Jesus!*
>
> *O clement, O loving, O sweet Virgin Mary! Pray for us, O Holy Mother of God. That we may be made worthy of the promises of Christ.*

Next say the "O God, Whose Only Begotten Son" prayer:

> *O God, Whose only begotten Son, by His life, death, and resurrection, has purchased for us the reward of eternal life; grant, we beseech Thee, that, meditating upon these mysteries of the Most Holy Rosary of the Blessed Virgin Mary, we may imitate what they contain and obtain what they promise. Through the same Christ our Lord. Amen. Mary, Queen of the Most Holy Rosary, pray for us.*

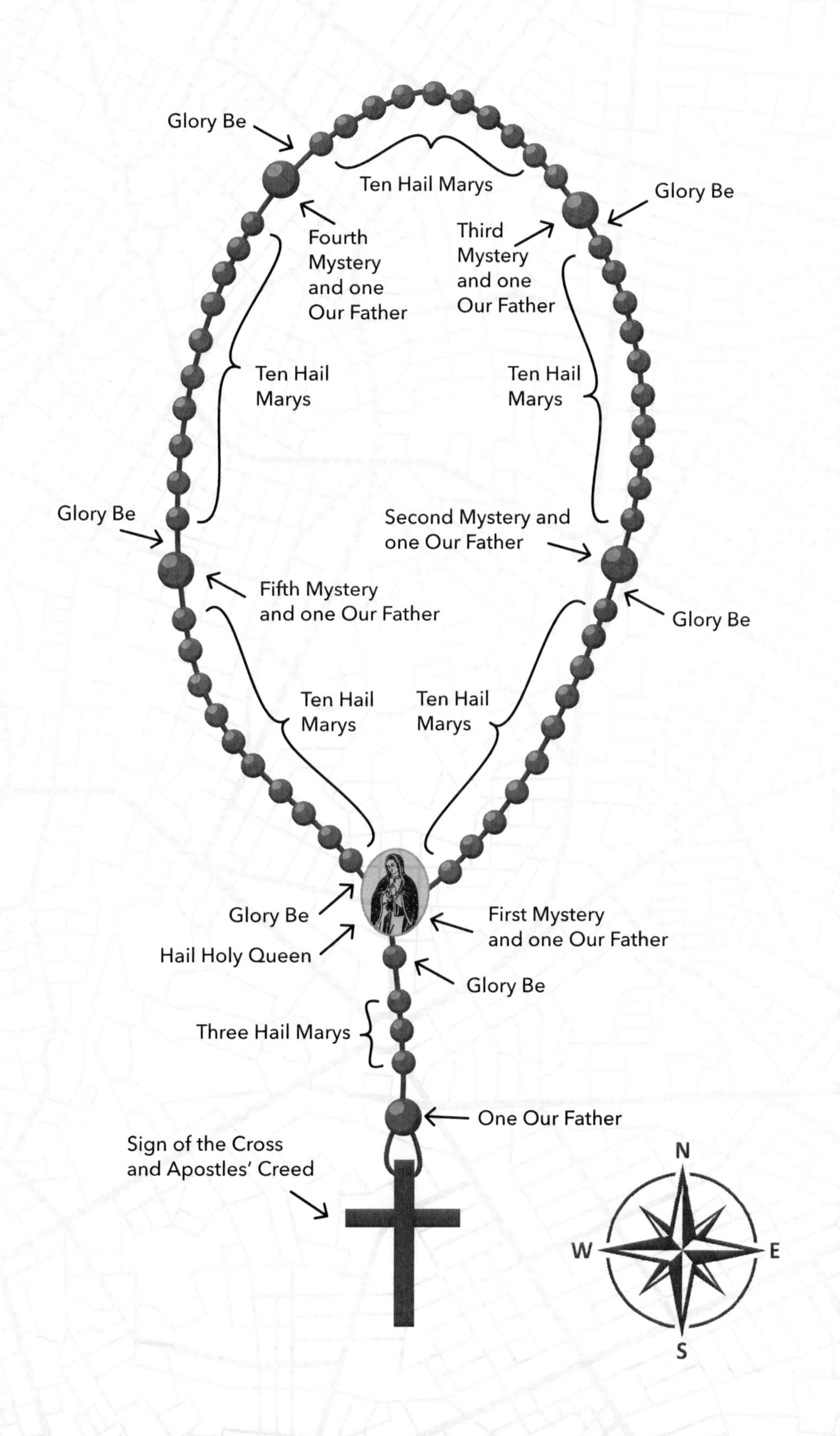
Glory Be
Ten Hail Marys
Glory Be
Fourth
Mystery
and one
Our Father
Third
Mystery
and one
Our Father
Ten Hail
Marys
Ten Hail
Marys
Glory Be
Second Mystery and
one Our Father
Fifth Mystery
and one Our Father
Glory Be
Ten Hail
Marys
Ten Hail
Marys
Glory Be
Hail Holy Queen
First Mystery
and one Our Father
Glory Be
Three Hail Marys
One Our Father
Sign of the Cross
and Apostles' Creed
N
W
E
S

The next two prayers are special to our family. They are not a part of the Rosary but did indeed help us on our journey of healing. We always prayed them together at the end of the Rosary. They have a personal connection to Mary Ellen.

> *O God, our Creator and Redeemer, we humbly adore You. We thank you for our lives, our joys, and for the crosses that have made us strong. Realizing Your special love for children, in Your words: "Suffer the little children to come unto Me and forbid them not, for such is the Kingdom of Heaven," we now ask You to hear the prayers we humbly offer You, through Your beloved Mary Ellen Le Brun. Help us to imitate her childlike faith, sincere love, and prayerful enthusiasm for doing Your will in all things, calling to mind Your words, "Unless you become as little children, you shall not enter the Kingdom of Heaven...."*

> *Dear Mary Ellen, beloved by God, companion now of all the angels and saints, we turn our thoughts to you in heaven and earnestly ask you to hear us. Kindly place this special intention before God, and above all, help us to obtain final perseverance throughout our trials and sufferings, so that when the journey of life is over, we too, may enter God's Kingdom, to enjoy eternal peace and happiness with you and all His angels and saints, through Christ our Lord. Amen.*

Traditionally, after loved ones pass you pray for them while they journey to their next life. Safe passage, safe landing perhaps. Many people have referred to my sister as a saint and pray for her canonization. No doubt her journey was a holy one. I believe many people who have touched lives in transforming ways are saintly. I know she continues to affect from there to here. Because of this my family and I and many others pray to her because we believe she intercedes for us.

## IN HEAVEN WE'LL UNDERSTAND

Not now, but in the coming years
It may be in the heavenly land,
We'll read the meaning of our tears;
Some day in heaven, we'll understand.

We'll know why clouds instead of sun
Were over a cherished plan.
Why smiles have ceased when just began.
Some day in heaven we'll understand.

Then trust in God, through all thy days,
Fear not for he doth hold thy hand.
But, whilst you live, still sing and praise,
Some day in heaven we'll understand.

Author Unknown

# Epilogue

I see you. I feel you. I am you.

I am that little girl reeling from trauma and wondering what happened to her sister and when was she coming back? I was given the keys but I'm too young to drive. Hail Mary, I am four.

I am that middle school kid still trying to adjust to loss. Grieving but not knowing. Managing teenage angst and girl drama and wish you were here to help me navigate this bumpy road. I am behind the wheel with no license to drive. Hail Mary, I am twelve.

I am the high school cheerleader living a happy life. Grief weaves in and out like traffic. Feelings of loss are intermittent. I have my driver's license now and can't wait to get behind the wheel. No sense of direction, though. Can't read a map. I get lost a lot. Hail Mary, I am sixteen.

I am the college coed and there is a loneliness I don't understand. Still swallowed up in loss. Wondering why I was spared. I am running low on gas most of the time. And spending too much time tailgating. No one drives fast enough for me. Spending a lot of time doing donuts in the parking lot.

Not enjoying the drive but wanting to get to the destination. Unknowing that the trip is long and never ending. Hail Mary, I am twenty.

I am working my first job and begin to feel lost. What's my purpose and my direction? Where am I driving and why am I speeding all the time? Life is fast and I am in a hurry going through it. I need to slow down but my pedal is to the metal. I start to write this book. Hail Mary, I am twenty-two.

I am a bride getting ready to marry the love of my life. Lala, you are always missed in the big and small moments. I begin to go the speed limit and navigate the curves of the road. Hail Mary, I am twenty-eight.

I become a mom and am injected with joy and worry of knowing what can happen. It can be paralyzing. Time to get a bigger more family-oriented car. It becomes filled with infant and toddler car seats, sippy cups, and stale Cheerios crumbs. I become aware of my journey and the drive. It's not just me anymore. Hail Mary, I am thirty-six.

I feel a camaraderie being a mom with my parents. The unpacking gets more intense as I begin to understand their loss, our loss. Afraid to hold on and scared to let go. I am beginning to slow down; take in the scenery. My parents and I don't drive the same car. I hope that I never do. Hail Mary, I am forty.

I believe without hesitation that you, Lala, put lifelong sisters in my path at every turn, from kindergarten, third grade, high school, college, my first job, mothers on the playground and the little league field. And those sisters who serendipitously showed up and never left. Then there are those with whom we discover we have shared sister stories of loss. We were meant to find one another. We form lifelong bonds of solidarity. We remember and talk of our sisters. Healing continues. Unpacking years of grief begins to require a large bed pickup truck. You have seen to it that I am never sisterless. These women have affected my life in ways I know you would have, and I am forever grateful and blessed. Hail Mary, I am any age.

I am the silver stage of my life, and I am a woman who has grieved the loss of her sister for more than half of her life. Missing you never ends, but I feel the intensity of your spirit now more than ever. This book has been instrumental in my grief since I first took the keys way back when. I've been driving a long time. My car is cleaner, smaller, and less cluttered. Kids are in college now; they drive their own cars. I try to keep the tank full, take the car for regular maintenance or whatever big repair comes my way. Grief trains you for the long drive, prepares you for the never-ending journey until it just becomes a part of you. I don't deserve it, but I guess I've earned it. Hail Mary, I am fifty-seven.

# Notes


1 Father Frank Taney, Mary Ellen's New Rosary for Young People, (Staten Island, NY: St. Paul's Publications, 1970).

2 Elisabeth Kubler-Ross, On Death and Dying, (New York: Macmillan Publishing, 1969).

3 Ali Ibn Hassan, "Mary in the Quran", February 2, 2018, https://www.catholic.com/magazine/online-edition/mary-in-the-quran.

4 Rolling Stones, "You Can't Always Get What You Want", *Let It Bleed,* London Records, London, recorded November 16-17, 1968.

5 Elizabeth Kelly, "The Rosary as a Tool for Meditation", Loyolapress.com, https://www.loyolapress.com/catholic-resources/prayer/personal-prayer-life/different-ways-to-pray/the-rosary-as-a-tool-for-meditation-by-liz-kelly/.

# Acknowledgments

To my uncle, Fr. Frank Taney, for your unconventional spirit and your original creation of *Mary Ellen's New Rosary for Young People*, you were the architect of shifting an antiquated prayer into a renewed classic. You have eternally inspired me to promote it further with *Holy Shift!*, hailing Mary. I feel your angel smiles upon me. Your passing in November 2001 has us all missing your positive energy.

For my sister, Mary Ellen, I am eternally connected to you. You are the reason I have been able to create an entanglement of loss and prayer. Neither could exist without the other. You continue to be the brightest star in the night sky. I look for you there always. You are the best example of why doing the right thing matters.

To my parents, Alice and Louis Le Brun, your steadfast courage is awe-inspiring. Thank you for encouraging me to create this sequel to a lovely first. Dad, I love and miss you every day. You were my first Prince Charming, and you will be my forever hero. You saved our family after loss, were the injector of joy after sorrow, and a fine example of what reliance on faith is capable of. Your dedication and love to our family is an example everyone should emulate. Upon your passing in 2018, I am sure that your heavenly reunion with Mary Ellen was nothing short of magnificent. During your eulogy, Steve said, "Lou was the glue." You most definitely were, and life is a little untethered without you. Every time I hear "*Michelle, ma belle*" I know you are close.

Mom, I will always be grateful for your unwavering and steadfast support all my life and especially during this project. Your constant encouragement is priceless. You have my eternal admiration and respect for surviving such a tragedy and still have deep faith. Your dedication has rewarded you with great grace to carry this lifelong cross. You are the spackle to our faith, always filling in the cracks so we don't crumble. Mom, I will always be in awe of you and love you forever.

For my brothers, Dave and Steve, for generously providing personal, raw, and heartfelt reflections. This version would be incomplete without you. Being your kid sister was pure joy while growing up with Mary Ellen in the rearview mirror, only to realize she was a driving force in our lives. Thank you for always looking out for me until I could look out for myself. I love you both and your beautiful families; no doubt Mary Ellen smiles down on you.

To my husband, Elbert, I thank you for always inspiring us to start each day anew and, as my mom always says, "for being a better Catholic than me." Quite a compliment for an Episcopalian who has always supported, encouraged, and helped sustain faith in our family and our home. I love you and our crazy big love and no matter what, our hearts no doubt will find each other in the next life.

To my twins, Margaux and Michael, you are my opus. I believe Mary Ellen's legacy runs through your veins. I hope you feel fortified with her unique superpower, the desire to always "right the wrongs of this life." And as you face your life challenges, I hope an instilled faith will serve you well. ILU2TM&B is an understatement.

To the friends and family who contributed their connections to Mary Ellen, they are the example of how one life can touch another's forever. Your thoughts demonstrate how shared love never dies.

To my handpicked flowers and old souls who kept pushing me to write this, you know who you are; you've cried with me, laughed with me, shared with me your strength to persevere and to push "send."

And to all those spiritual angels and those living old souls still waiting for wings, you know who you are. So many have been purposeful in this second creation. I am eternally grateful and blessed to have so many God winks, angel flutters, or serendipitous moments. Nothing is by accident. It's a divine plan. And it forces us to detour because sometimes you must get lost to be found. Because when I say it takes faith, family, and friends to endure loss, that is truly an understatement. I have the trifecta of blessings.

To Robin Ryan, who felt strongly in supporting me to create this legacy to my sister and for introducing me to Henry DeVries and his staff from Indie Books International, who guided me in my "mess to success." To my managing editor Lisa Lucas: we were meant to meet and work together. Kindred souls from a vintage time. A God wink, for sure. To my brother from another mother, Brad Backman, for helping me to create the cover of my dreams. I feel our sisters rejoicing.

# About The Author

Michelle Le Brun has been a writer since she could hold a pen. Besides boho clothing, wine, and cooking, writing is her fanatical passion. She has the gift of injecting meaning into raw emotion. Michelle is blessed with the ability to express feelings with fancy. Her friends joke that she should write eulogies as a side hustle, demonstrating the depth of loss she's experienced in her life and her innate ability to intimately know someone and put that relationship into words.

Her fifteen minutes of fame was working at the White House, serving President Reagan as a member of his presidential speechwriting office from 1987–89. She was a proud member of the president's kazoo playing "Balcony Gang." When the Reagans left the White House, she did too and went down the street to Capitol Hill to work for a California Congressman.

Michelle missed her roots and moved back to where she grew up in the beautiful Finger Lakes in upstate New York. She enjoyed working in public relations until she got bit by the wine bug in 1997 and has been a fine wine consultant ever since. She holds a BA in journalism.

She and her husband, Elbert Eller, married in 1994. Their twins, Margaux and Michael, were born in the shadow of 9/11 but stand in the sun pursuing their college endeavors and career paths. She admits even the best marriage can be hard but rewarding when you are both passionate personalities but being a mama bear is the toughest job of all. She would not change either as both are a blessed privilege. Her parents, Alice and Louis, were excellent role models for both. On the same day she and Elbert became empty nesters, their next furry child was born. Dolce, their chocolate lab, aka "the chocolate beast," has settled in nicely at their cottage on Cayuga Lake.

Michelle is fiercely devoted to her family and her friends. She's French and Irish by descent so she will love and forgive but is a bit of a grudger. She knows she is strong willed so save your breath. Her favorite collection are the old souls in her life. Her friends are handpicked, and her bouquet is filled with wildflowers.

Making people laugh with a reality check brings her joy. Her heart is huge, and she loves big, but she won't let you wallow in $#!t too long. She will never let you know what she's thinking, but she will always speak her mind. This is her truth. *Holy Shift!* is her first published book as she's been writing it most of her life. And her yellow 1967 VW stick shift convertible Bug? Michelle admits, she and Sweet Pea are always a work in progress.

Made in United States
North Haven, CT
15 April 2023